CIVIL WAR DAYS

American Kids in History™

CIVIL WAR DAYS

Discover the Past with Exciting Projects, Games, Activities, and Recipes

David C. King

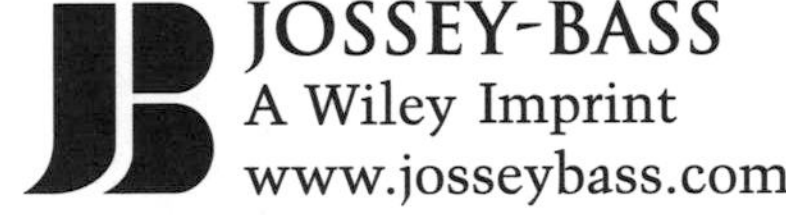
JOSSEY-BASS
A Wiley Imprint
www.josseybass.com

Published by Jossey-Bass
A Wiley Imprint
989 Market Street, San Francisco, CA 94103-1741 www.josseybass.com

Published simultaneously in Canada

Design: Michaelis/Carpelis Design Assoc., Inc.

Library of Congress Cataloging-in-Publication Data

King, David C.
Civil War days: discover the past with exciting projects, games, activities, and recipes / David C. King.
p. cm. — (American kids in history)
Includes bibliographical references and index.
Summary: Discusses what life was like for American during the Civil War; follows a year in the lives of two fictional families: a white family from the South and a black family from the North; and presents projects and activities from that time period.
ISBN 0-471-24612-3 (paper: alk. paper)
1. United States—History—Civil War, 1861–1865—Social aspects—Study and teaching—Activity programs—Juvenile literature.
2. United States—History—Civil War, 1861–1865—Children—Study and teaching—Activity programs—Juvenile literature.
3. Children—United States—Social life and customs—19th century—Study and teaching—Activity programs—Juvenile literature
[1. United States—History—Civil War, 1861–1865.
2. Afro-Americans—History—To 1862.] I. Title. II. Series.
E468.9.K56 1999
973.7—dc21 98-33657

Printed in the United States of America
FIRST EDITION
PB Printing 10 9

To my brother

ACKNOWLEDGMENTS

Special thanks to the many people who made this book possible, including: Kate C. Bradford, Joanne Palmer, Diane Aronson, and the editorial staff of the Professional and Trade Division, John Wiley & Sons, Inc.; Susan E. Meyer and the staff of Roundtable Press, Inc.; Marianne Palladino and Irene Carpelis of Michaelis/Carpelis Design; Miriam Sarzin, for her copy editing, Sharon Flitterman-King and Diane Ritch for craft expertise; Rona Tuccillo for picture research; Cheryl Kirk Noll for the drawings; Steven Tiger, librarian, and the students of the Roe-Jan Elementary School, Hillsdale, New York; and, for research assistance, the staff members of the Great Barrington Public Library, the Atheneum (Pittsfield, Massachusetts), Old Sturbridge Village, and the Farmers Museum, Cooperstown, New York. Historical photographs courtesy of Dover Publications, Inc.

CONTENTS

INTRODUCTION

The Civil War, 1861–1865

In the 1800s, the American nation became deeply and bitterly divided over slavery. Slavery had ended in the states of the North and the West, but it remained in the South, where more than four million people of African descent lived as slaves. The owners of large Southern farms called plantations owned most of the slaves, using them to work huge fields of cotton, tobacco, rice, and sugar.

While the South remained a region of small farms and sprawling plantations, the North was becoming a region of bustling cities and large factories, or mills. Southerners preferred their slower, more rural way of life, and most of them believed that way of life depended on slavery. As the population and wealth of the North grew, Southerners feared that the government would be controlled by the North and could force them to free their slaves.

To protect slavery, eleven Southern states declared they would no longer be part of the United States. Instead, they announced they were forming a new nation called the Confederate States of America. People in the other twenty-three states said that the nation is a permanent union of states and must remain united. The Civil War began in April 1861. Southerners fought to preserve their way of life, including slavery. Northerners fought to restore the unity of the nation.

During four years of fighting, many Southern children grew up with the war close at hand. Battles raged across their families' farms and through the streets of their towns. Every family had young men proudly serving in the gray uniforms of the Confederate armies. In the North, most children lived far from the boom of cannons and the crack of rifles, but they watched fathers and brothers, uncles and cousins march off to war in the dark blue uniforms of the North, or Union.

In 1862, President Abraham Lincoln issued a statement called the Emancipation Proclamation, declaring that all slaves in the Confederate states still at war would be officially free on January 1, 1863. Northerners were now fighting for great goals: restoring the nation and ending slavery. Both goals were achieved when the Civil War finally ended in April 1865.

The Parkhursts and the Wheelers

The Parkhursts and the Wheelers are not real families, but their stories show what life might have been like for a Southern family and a Northern family during the Civil War years.

Eleven-year-old Emily Parkhurst lived in Charleston, South Carolina, one of the few large towns in the South. Her parents, Frederick and Louise Parkhurst, owned a small business shipping cotton from plantations to mills in the North and in England. The mills turned the raw cotton into fabric for clothing, table cloths, sheets, and other things. Like many white families in the South, the Parkhursts were opposed to slavery, but they supported the Confederacy because they felt a deep loyalty to their state and region. When Emily's brother Ned turned seventeen, he joined a South Carolina regiment. The first part of this book follows Emily and her family through the spring and summer of 1862.

In spite of the hardships of the war, Emily's life was fairly normal. She went to a school for girls and she helped her mother with the cooking and housework. Although the war caused shortages of many things, Emily and her friends enjoyed making their own toys and games and found other ways to have fun.

The second part of the book follows the Wheeler family through the autumn and winter of 1862. Solomon and Hannah Wheeler had escaped from slavery in 1849 and made their way north to a New York City neighborhood where many former slaves and other free African Americans lived. Hannah Wheeler worked in a neighborhood general store and Solomon was a dock worker, loading and unloading ships.

Their son Timothy had just turned twelve and their daughter Lisa was six years old. Tim went to a school for African American children. Because both his parents worked, he often looked after Lisa and helped his grandmother Esther prepare meals and clean their small apartment. Tim was proud that his father wanted to join the Union army as soon as men of African descent were allowed to enlist.

The Projects and Activities

What would it be like to grow up during the Civil War? In this book, you'll take part in many of the same activities young people like Emily Parkhurst and Tim and Lisa Wheeler enjoyed in 1862, including baking hardtack, sending messages in Morse Code, and playing games brought to America by slaves from Africa. You can complete the projects and activities with materials you have around your home or school, or that can easily be purchased at very little cost. As you do the projects, activities, and recipes, you'll feel the past come alive and you'll discover what it was like to be an American kid in Civil War days.

CHAPTER ONE

SPRING

PRESSED-FLOWER SCRAPBOOK

PAPIER MÂCHÉ BOWL

TOY PARACHUTE

DECORATED BANDBOX

HARDTACK

GINGERBREAD

PAPER ART

In the spring of 1862, the Union navy formed a blockade of ships around Charleston Harbor. Emily and her family could often hear cannons booming as the forts guarding the city fired at the ships.

With the harbor blocked, the Parkhursts could no longer ship cotton from the plantations to mills in England. Papa Parkhurst bought looms for spinning the cotton into thread to set up their own mill. Anything the Parkhursts could make would help reduce the South's shortage of cloth.

Emily liked all the excitement of starting a mill. People came from all over South Carolina to help, and this meant there were often guests for dinner or overnight. She enjoyed helping Mama Parkhurst and their cook, Grace, prepare meals for the company. Then she could watch the guests work with Mama and Papa designing things like shirts and pants for soldiers.

EMILY'S GARDEN

The Parkhursts lived in a comfortable brick house in the center of Charleston, only two streets away from the harbor. Like most of their neighbors, the family enjoyed gardening, especially in the small courtyard behind the house. They also placed potted plants with colorful blossoms on the balconies that faced the street. The balconies had beautiful railings made of wrought iron in delicate shapes.

Because Mama was so busy with the cotton mill, she placed Emily in charge of the garden. Every day after school, Emily spent time transplanting seedlings, pulling weeds, and cutting flowers to decorate the house. The Parkhursts' young cook, Grace, was an immigrant from Ireland who knew a lot about gardening. With her help, the courtyard was soon full of blossoms of every size, shape, and color. Grace showed Emily how to make a plant press so she could save some of the prettiest spring blossoms. Emily pasted some of the pressed flowers into a scrapbook, and she and Grace used others to make notecards and framed pictures. They also made papier mâché bowls for displaying fresh-cut blossoms.

PROJECT PRESSED-FLOWER SCRAPBOOK

You can use pressed flowers for many different projects, including notecards, framed pictures, and bookmarks. In this project, you'll make a simple plant press and use some of the blossoms to make a scrapbook. This is a great way to keep a record of wildflowers you find on hikes, family vacations, or picnics. You can buy—or borrow from the library—a field guide to wildflowers to help you identify and label the plants you collect. Once the blossoms are pressed and dried, they will keep most of their color for many months.

Whenever possible, pick flowers late in the morning on a dry day, after the dew has evaporated and before the sun is hot. When you pick garden flowers or wildflowers on someone's property, always ask permission and take only as much as you need. Keep in mind that most state and national parks prohibit the picking of flowers, but fields, vacant lots, and even roadsides (away from traffic) will offer a surprising abundance for your collection.

MATERIALS

scissors with blunt or rounded tips
basket or grocery bag
several sheets of newspaper
paper towels
6 to 10 sheets of construction paper
2 pieces of stiff cardboard, about 9 by 12 inches
4 or 5 thick hardcover books
scrapbook or spiral notebook, 8½ by 11 inches or larger
white glue
pencil

1. Use blunt-tip scissors and a basket or grocery bag to cut and collect your flowers. Pick only one or two examples of each plant you find. Make a clean cut on the stem at a slight angle. Include two or three leaves and a little of the stem. *Note: Flowers with thick blossoms, like roses, don't press well, but you may want to use some of the petals for the color.*

2. Back indoors, spread newspaper over your work area and empty the basket or bag. If the blossoms or leaves are damp, blot them gently with paper towels.

3. Place a few blossoms, stems, and leaves on a sheet of construction paper. Spread out the pieces so they don't touch, and press down on any thick blossoms with your thumb. You may be able to fit three or four blossoms, with stems and leaves,

Flower Art for Girls

The daughters of well-to-do families in the 1860s usually went to private schools. The schools were called "young ladies' academies." The girls, ranging in age from seven to seventeen, studied reading, writing, penmanship, arithmetic, geography, history, and art. One of the most popular forms of art instruction was painting or drawing trees and flowers. Instead of bringing real flowers into the classroom, however, the teacher had the students copy pictures in books, like one called *Drawing Book of Flowers and Fruits.*

Parents were proud of their daughters' artwork, and they often paid high prices to have drawings and paintings framed by professional framers. A family's display of their young daughter's art was an indication that she was well educated.

on a single sheet of construction paper, but with larger plants you may need an entire sheet for one plant.

4. Place a second sheet of construction paper on top of the first. Add more blossoms, leaves, and stems to complete a second layer. Continue to add more layers until you have samples of each of the plants you collected.

5. Make a simple plant press by placing your stack of flowers and construction paper between the two pieces of stiff cardboard. Put this in a warm, dry location and place the pile of hardcover books on top. Allow 2 or 3 weeks for the blossoms to press and dry.

6. When the flowers are dry and have been pressed flat, carefully take the press apart. Cover your work area with newspaper and gently spread the dried flowers on it.

7. Choose one of each type of flower to place in your scrapbook. On each page of the scrapbook, arrange the blossom, stem, and leaves of one plant. Use a dab of white glue to fix the pieces to the page.

8. Put different varieties of flowers on separate pages. If you know the name of each flower, or can find it in a field guide, write the name at the bottom of the page. Also write the date you found it and the location. Keep adding to your scrapbook through the summer and autumn.

PROJECT PAPIER MÂCHÉ BOWL

Papier mâché is a French term that means "mashed paper." It's a mixture of paper and paste that can be molded like clay into all sorts of shapes. The basic paste, or mash, is easy to make and you'll find it's fun to work with. In some papier mâché techniques, the paper is ground into tiny bits and added to the mash. For your papier mâché bowl, you'll use strips of paper dipped in the mash, and then you'll paint the finished bowl.

You can use any kind of paper that absorbs well for your mash, including paper towels, newspaper, tissue paper, or grocery bags. Papers that are shiny, like magazine pages, don't work well because they don't absorb the paste.

MATERIALS

measuring cup
tea kettle
3 cups water
medium-size saucepan, about 2 quarts
½ cup flour
1 cup cold water
mixing spoon
paper towels, newspaper, or other absorbent scrap paper
several sheets of newspaper
ruler
small, smooth bowl to use as a mold (a plastic tub for butter or margarine works well)
petroleum jelly
¼ teaspoon oil of cloves or oil of wintergreen (optional)
small storage jar with lid (optional)
table knife
fine-grit sandpaper (optional)
poster paint or acrylic paint, your choice of 1 or 2 colors
small paintbrush
adult helper

1. Ask your adult helper to heat about 3 cups of water in the kettle, bringing it to a gentle boil.

2. While the water is heating, measure the flour into the saucepan. Slowly stir in about 1 cup of cold tap water. Continue stirring until all lumps are removed and the mixture is completely blended and smooth.

3. Have the adult stir in about 1½ cups of the hot water. Stir until completely blended. If the paste seems very thick, add a little more hot water.

4. Ask the adult to cook the mixture over medium heat for 2 to 3 minutes, with occasional stirring. Turn off the heat and let the mixture cool for 15 to 20 minutes.

5. While the papier mâché paste cools, tear sheets of newspaper, paper towels, or scraps into strips about ½ inch wide and 4 to 6 inches long. You'll need between 30 and 50 strips.

Hint: You'll find the strips are easier to tear if you tear along the edge of a ruler.

6. Spread several sheets of newspaper over your work surface. Place the bowl or butter tub upside down on the newspaper. Smear petroleum jelly over the outside of the bowl, covering it completely with a thin film. This will prevent the papier mâché from sticking to the bowl or tub.

7. Dip a strip of paper into the papier mâché paste, soaking it completely. Pull the strip between your fingers to remove the excess paste, as shown in the picture.

8. Press the pasted strip onto the outside of the bowl. Continue applying pasted strips to the bowl, overlapping the edges, until the bowl is completely covered by a layer of strips. As you apply each pasted strip, smooth it down with your fingers to remove any bumps or air bubbles.

9. Apply 4 or 5 more layers of pasted strips the same way. The bowl will be stronger if you apply each layer of strips in a different direction or in a criss-cross pattern.

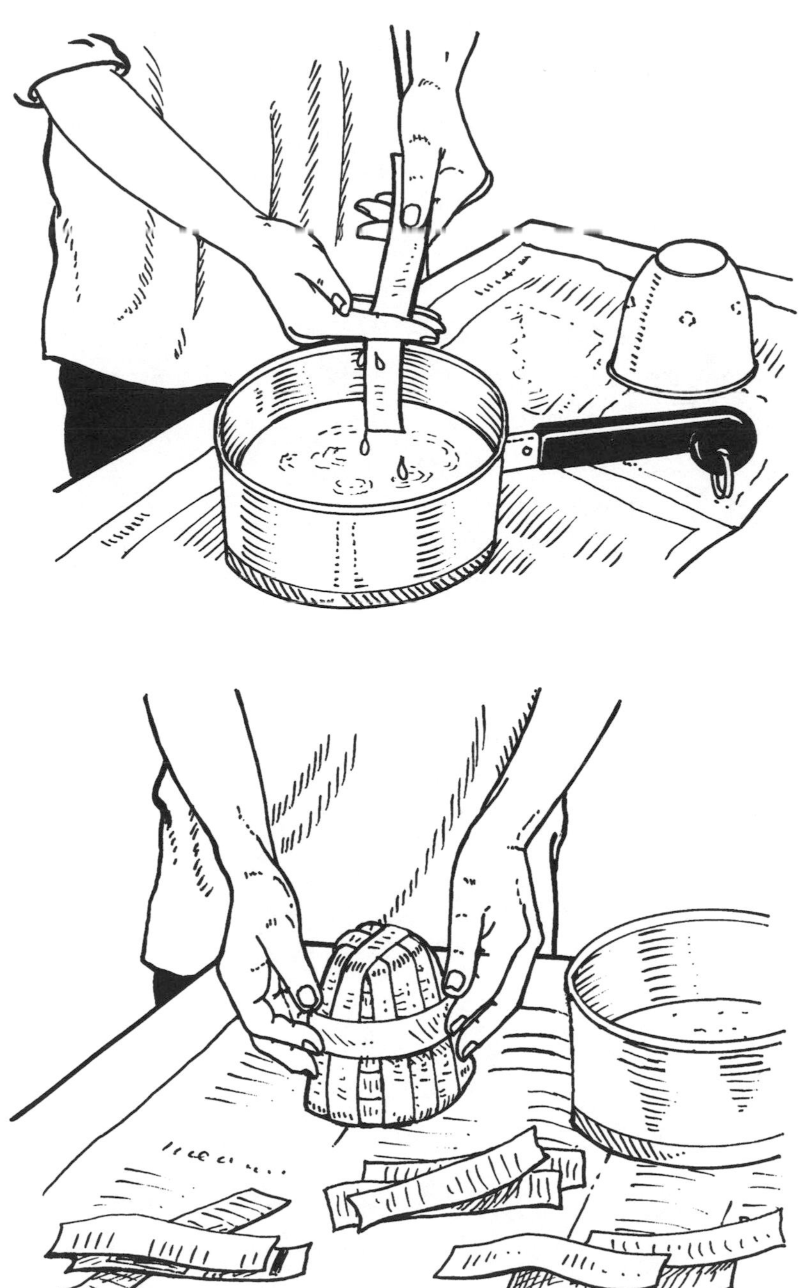

The Many Uses of Papier Mâché

Although papier mâché is a French term, this material was developed by the Chinese about 2,000 years ago—not long after they invented paper. By the mid-1800s, artists and craftspeople had devised many different uses for this unusual material. In addition to bowls, they made papier mâché boxes, trays, toys, and even items of furniture like chests and stools. In the 1860s, a department store in New York City attracted large crowds with a window display of life-size papier mâché figures in Christmas scenes. American toy makers in the 1860s used papier mâché to make puppets and dolls with movable heads and arms.

10. Remove any leftover paste from the saucepan with the mixing spoon. If the paste has begun to harden, add a little water. If you have a lot of paste left over, add the oil of cloves or wintergreen, stir, and store the paste in a covered jar to use in other projects. (The paste can be stored for 2 to 3 weeks.)

11. Allow the papier mâché to dry completely for 4 or 5 days before you remove it from the mold. If your papier mâché bowl doesn't come off the mold easily, insert a table knife between the mold and the papier mâché and gently pry it off.

12. If you want to make the outside of your bowl smoother, you can sand the rough spots with a fine-grit sandpaper. Wipe off the sandpaper dust with a paper towel before painting.

13. Paint your bowl inside and out with poster paint or acrylic paint in your choice of color or colors. For decoration, paint the bowl in one color, allow the paint to dry (about 1 hour for poster paint, less for acrylics), then apply a design in another color or colors. Use your completed bowl to store paper clips, coins, or other objects.

Note: In order to use the bowl for food or liquid, you would have to coat it further with asphaltum, available at craft and hobby stores.

A PLANTATION VISIT

Early in April, the Parkhursts rode the family carriage to a plantation almost fifty miles from Charleston. The plantation, which covered more than 1,000 acres, was owned by Emily's Uncle Ross and Aunt Margaret. Emily was very fond of her aunt and uncle and their son Alexander, who was twelve years old. And she loved the great house with its spacious rooms and breezy porches.

Sometimes, however, Emily was troubled by the idea that more than forty slaves worked the fields of cotton and rice or worked as household servants. Emily's parents had taught her that it was wrong for people to own other human beings. Like many white families, however, the Parkhursts believed that one day the slaves would be freed; but they also felt that the North had no right to interfere with the way Southerners did things.

The week on the plantation passed quickly. Emily and her cousin Alexander played croquet on the lawn and Aunt Margaret helped Emily make a bandbox to use when she traveled. Alexander also showed Emily how to make a toy parachute that they played with so much it finally fell apart.

PROJECT TOY PARACHUTE

Even though the Wright brothers did not make the first airplane flight until 1903, people in the 1800s were fascinated by the idea of flying. Daring "aeronauts" in Europe and America had been riding hot-air balloons since the late 1700s, and other daredevils had been jumping off cliffs and buildings with parachutes nearly as long. No one knows who invented the first toy parachute, but they were popular with children throughout the 1800s. Some even designed ways to send the parachute aloft with a kite, then have it release to drift slowly to the ground. While young people in the 1800s usually made their toy parachutes out of lightweight canvas, you'll make yours with a piece of cotton.

MATERIALS

14-inch square of cotton or other lightweight fabric
hole punch or large nail
about 60 inches of thin, strong string, like kite string
4 metal washers, ¾-to-1-inch across (available for a few cents at any hardware department and many supermarkets)

1. Fold in each corner of the cloth square to form 4 small triangles, as shown in the picture. Use a hole punch or large nail to make a hole through both layers of fabric in each corner triangle.

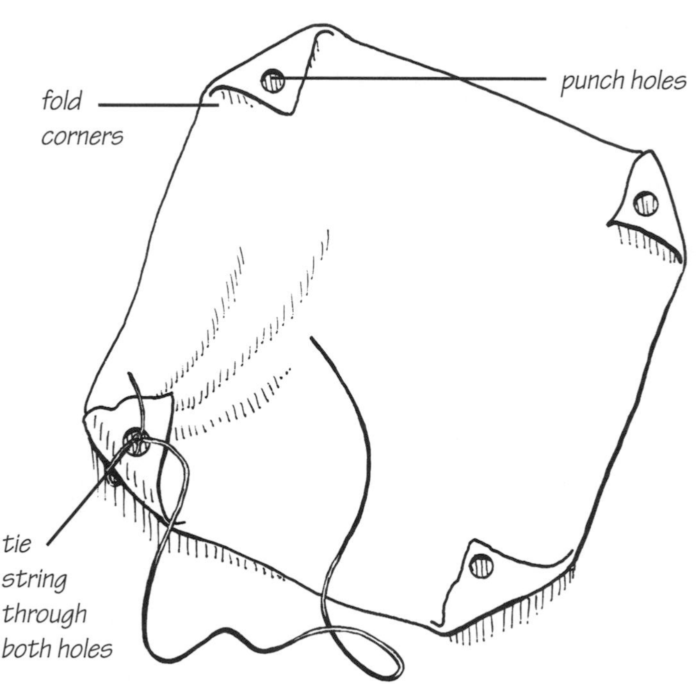

2. Cut four pieces of string, each 14 inches long. Run a piece of string through the double hole in each corner and tie it to the edge of the fabric in a firm double knot.

3. Place the 4 washers on top of each other in a stack. Tie the ends of all four strings to the stack of washers, as shown in the picture. Be careful not to tangle the strings.

4. Carefully fold the sides of the parachute toward the center. Again, make sure the strings don't become tangled. Place the pile of washers on top and fold the cloth over them in a neat package.

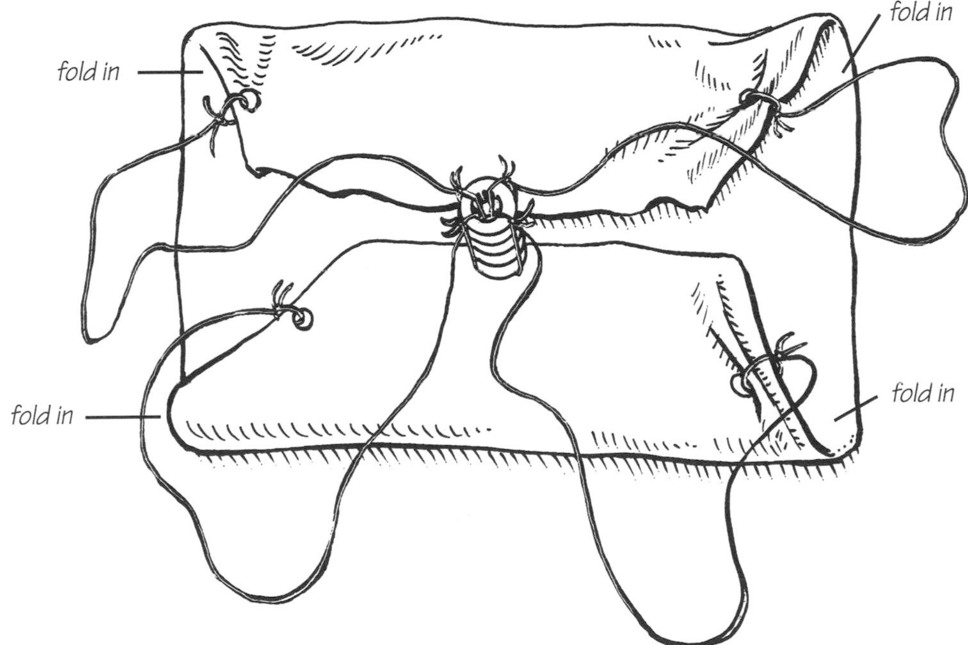

Professor Lowe's Hot-Air Balloons

One evening in 1861, people in South Carolina were startled when a huge hot-air balloon landed in a farm field. Soldiers captured the man in the balloon's gondola and held him as a spy for the North. The balloonist explained that his name was Professor Thaddeus Lowe and that he had been blown off course on a flight from Cincinnati, Ohio, more than 900 miles away.

Lowe's experience in South Carolina gave him an idea: After he was released by the Confederate soldiers, he went to Washington, D.C., and offered his services to the Union. President Abraham Lincoln made Lowe the nation's first "aeronaut," and you could say this was the nation's first "air corps." During the Civil War, Professor Lowe made many balloon flights for the Union army, reporting on the position of the Confederate forces. On some occasions, he even used a telegraph to send messages from his balloon gondola to army headquarters.

5. Your parachute is now ready. Take it outdoors away from trees, overhead wires, or other obstacles. Throw your parachute package as high in the air as you can. The package will unwrap and the parachute will open as it drifts slowly to the ground. (If the parachute comes down too fast, remove one of the washers.)

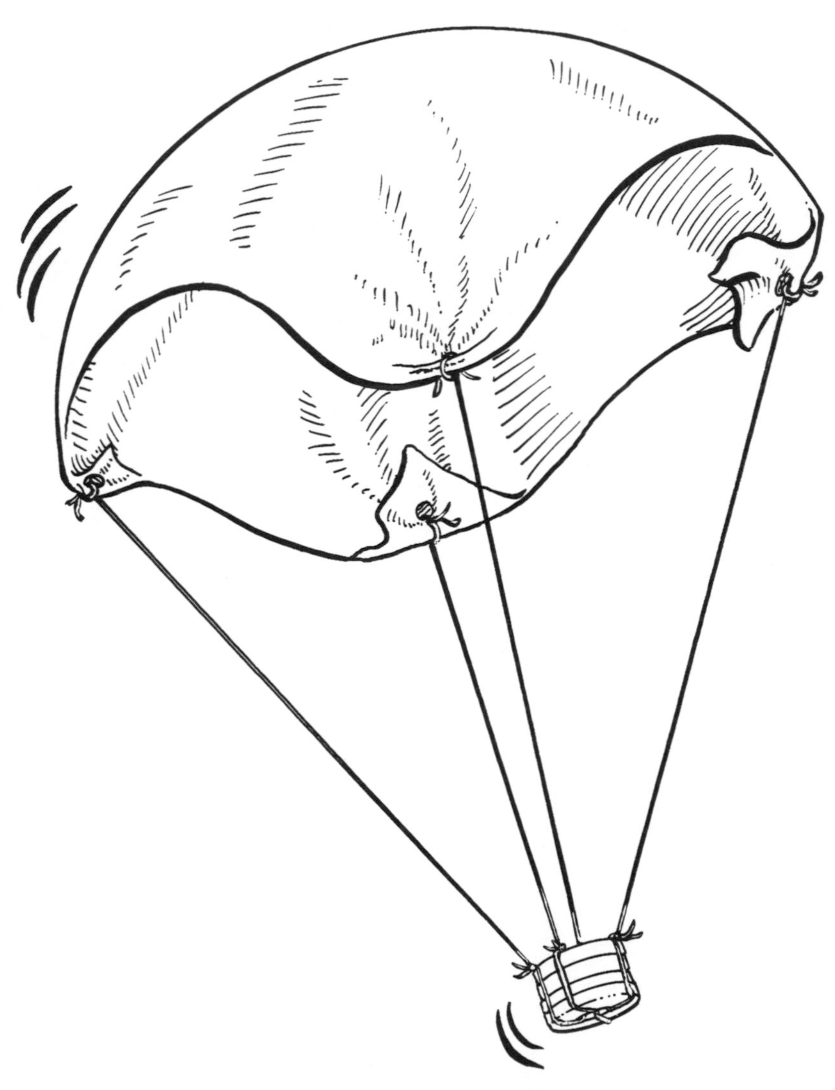

PROJECT DECORATED BANDBOX

When people traveled in the 1800s, they used bandboxes to carry things like hats, gloves, scarves, and jewelry. The first bandboxes, made of thin wood, were used by manufacturers in the late 1700s to ship men's shirt collars, called bands, to the customer. People found the boxes were attractive and convenient for storage and travel. They lined the insides of the boxes with newspaper and decorated the outsides with colorful wallpaper. By the late 1860s, as travel by railroad became common, the lightweight boxes were often banged up in the baggage cars, and so bandboxes were gradually replaced by sturdier luggage. Bandboxes are still popular today for storage or as gift boxes.

Bandboxes came in all sizes and shapes, but round or oval boxes were the most popular. For your bandbox, you'll use an empty round oatmeal container, but you can use the same technique on any sturdy cardboard box—round, square, or rectangular. To cover the box, you can use either wallpaper or heavyweight wrapping paper. You can buy wallpaper remnants for a few cents at wall-covering stores or the home decorating section of many discount department stores.

MATERIALS

several sheets of newspaper
empty round oatmeal box, or similar container
tape measure
pencil
wallpaper or gift wrapping paper (about 36 by 36 inches)
ruler
scissors
white glue
piece of sponge
cloth ribbon, ½ to 1 inch wide, about 20 inches long, any solid color
transparent tape (optional)

1. Spread several sheets of newspaper over your work surface.

2. Use the tape measure to measure the distance around the box, the perimeter, and the height. (The perimeter of a standard 18-ounce oatmeal box is 12½ inches and the height is 7 inches.)

3. Place the wallpaper or wrapping paper, design-side down, on your work surface. With ruler and pencil, mark a piece of paper as long as the perimeter of the box, plus 1 inch for overlap, and as wide as the box is high. For a standard oatmeal box, the paper should measure 13½ by 7 inches. Cut out the piece of paper.

4. With the paper strip design-side down on your work surface, spread glue on the back of the strip. Use a piece of sponge dampened with water to spread the glue thinly and evenly over the entire surface.

5. Center the oatmeal container on the pasted strip. Make sure the top and bottom edges of the strip are lined up with the container's top and bottom edges. Carefully wrap the strip around the container. Use your fingers to smooth out any air bubbles that form.

6. To cover the lid, lay a piece of paper design-side down on your work surface. Place the lid on the paper and trace around the circle. Cut out the circle.

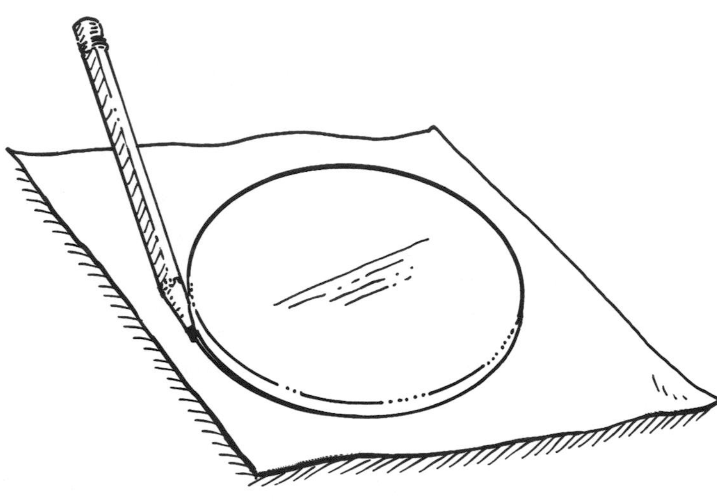

7. Spread glue on the back of the circle, using the piece of sponge. Paste the circle to the top of the lid, smoothing it out with your fingers.

8. The lids of most modern oatmeal boxes don't have sides that extend part way down the box. Older boxes do have lids with sides. If you have a box lid with sides, cover the ½ to 1-inch side the same way you did the sides of the container. Follow steps 3 through 5.

9. To add a ribbon to your bandbox, turn the container upside down. Paste or glue the middle part of a ribbon to the bottom of the box. The ribbon should be 2½ times the height of the box. (If the container is 8 inches high, the ribbon should be about 20 inches long.)

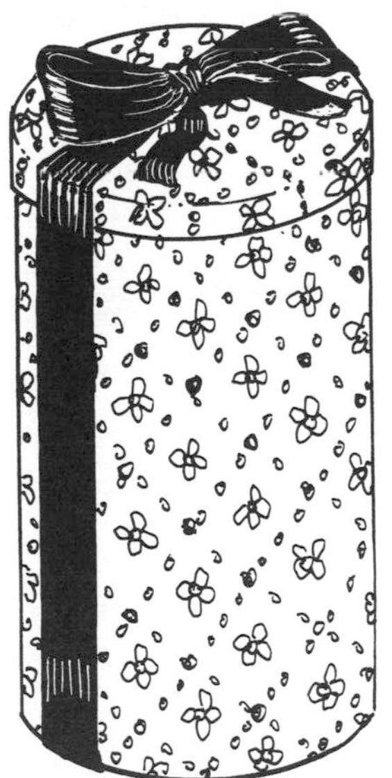

10. Run the ribbon up the sides of the box, gluing it to the sides. Stop gluing about 1½ inches from the top of the box. For extra strength, you can tape the ribbon to the box 1½ inches from the top.

11. With the lid on, bring the two ribbon ends over the top and tie a bow. Your decorated bandbox is now ready for storing your valuables or to give as a gift.

Bandboxes by "Aunt Hannah"

Bandboxes were very popular from the 1820s through the 1860s, especially with the young women who worked in the nation's fast-growing factories and mills. The most famous maker of bandboxes was a New Hampshire woman named Hannah Davis. From about 1825 to 1862, she traveled from town to town in a horse-drawn wagon loaded with her bandboxes. "Aunt Hannah," as she was known, made the boxes from thin pine or spruce wood that she bent into round or oval shapes. She made her own hand-printed papers and attached her business card inside each lid. She printed her name and the date on the card, along wih the words "Warranted Nailed Band Boxes." Many of Aunt Hannah's sturdy boxes have survived and are now in museum collections.

NED GOES TO WAR

Early in June 1862, Emily's brother Ned turned seventeen and his parents agreed that he could join the Confederate army. Ned was excited and immediately signed to serve with a South Carolina regiment. Mama and Papa Parkhurst were proud of him. He would be helping to defend Charleston and their state from being conquered by the North. The Parkhursts were opposed to slavery, but for them the important thing was to support their state.

Emily was proud of Ned, too, but she worried about how hard military life would be. As a going-away present, she made a picture of the beautiful South Carolina seacoast for him to look at when he felt homesick. She helped Grace and Mama bake gingerbread for him to share with his friends and a package of hardtack to add to his soldier's rations.

HARDTACK

Throughout the 1800s, hardtack was a common food for sailors and for pioneers heading west. This simple, hard biscuit was also known by many other names, including sea biscuit, trail bread, and ship's biscuit. During the Civil War, hardtack was a standard part of every soldier's rations. When the men were in camp, they often made their own, which was easy to do since all they needed was flour, water, and a touch of salt.

Making your own hardtack will give you a good idea of the plain foods soldiers ate. You'll probably find that hardtack is pretty tasteless, however, so you'll want to spread it with honey or jam.

INGREDIENTS

3¼ cups flour
2 teaspoons salt
1 cup water
honey or jam

EQUIPMENT

mixing bowl
mixing spoon
bread board or pastry cloth
rolling pin
table knife
meat skewer or large clean nail
cookie sheet
glass or plastic container with lid
adult helper

MAKES

12 biscuits

1. Preheat the oven to 375 degrees F.

2. Measure 3 cups of flour and the salt into the bowl. Add the water a little at a time, stirring constantly with the mixing spoon. When the dough becomes too thick to stir, continue mixing with your hands.

3. Knead the dough with your hands, working it with your fingers like a lump of clay. If the dough is sticky, add a little more flour. Or, if the dough seems powdery, add a little water. Shape the dough into a ball.

4. Sprinkle the remaining flour onto a bread board or pastry cloth and place the ball of dough on it.

5. With the rolling pin, roll out the dough into a 9-by-12-inch rectangle about ½ inch thick.

6. With the table knife, cut the dough into 3-inch squares.

A Soldier's Food

When an army was in camp, the soldiers usually had enough to eat, but the meals were not very exciting—dried beef or bacon, beans or peas, bread, and coffee. The officers enjoyed the best food. Some even brought their own cooks and personal servants. Food suppliers, called sutlers, set up tents in the camps where they sold eggs, coffee, and fresh meat, usually at high prices.

The rations were even more tiresome when the army was on the move. Each soldier carried hardtack, salt pork, coffee, and a little sugar and salt. To improve their diet, the men foraged, or lived off the land. They bought—or simply took—whatever crops and farm animals they could find.

7. Use the meat skewer or nail to poke about 12 holes in each square.

8. Place the squares on the cookie sheet and ask your adult helper to bake them for about 25 minutes. Start checking the hardtack after 20 minutes. It is done when it turns a light, golden brown.

9. Allow the hardtack to cool for a few minutes. Serve it with honey or jam.

10. Store the rest of the hardtack in a container with a lid.

PROJECT GINGERBREAD

Gingerbread was one of the most popular desserts in the 1860s. The cookie form of gingerbread, cut into figures like gingerbread men, was also becoming common. You'll make the cake form of gingerbread, following a recipe that has changed very little since Civil War times.

INGREDIENTS

½ cup butter
1 cup sugar
2 eggs
¾ cup boiling water
¾ cup dark molasses
2½ cups flour
2 teaspoons baking soda
½ teaspoon salt
2 teaspoons powdered ginger
1 cup heavy cream

EQUIPMENT

tea kettle
9-inch square baking pan
wax paper
large mixing bowl
mixing spoon
egg beater
toothpick or cake tester
serving plate
small mixing bowl
serving spoon
adult helper

MAKES

6 to 8 servings

1. Allow the butter and eggs to reach room temperature before you begin.

2. Preheat the oven to 350 degrees F. Ask your adult helper to have ¾ cup of boiling water ready.

3. Using a piece of wax paper, spread a thin layer of butter over the inside of the baking pan.

4. Place the rest of the butter in the large bowl and stir it with the mixing spoon until it becomes creamy. Add the sugar and continue stirring.

5. Add the two eggs and use the egg beater to beat the mixture until all the ingredients are blended.

6. Have the adult pour in the boiling water. Add the molasses. Stir with the spoon, or use the egg beater to mix the ingredients.

7. Slowly stir in the flour, baking soda, salt, and ginger. Mix the batter thoroughly with the spoon.

8. Pour the batter into the buttered pan and bake for 35 to 40 minutes. Test by poking a toothpick or cake tester into the center of the cake. When the tester or toothpick comes out clean (with no batter sticking to it), the gingerbread is done.

9. Let the gingerbread cool in the pan for about 10 minutes, then turn it out onto a serving plate. While it is cooling, wash and dry the egg beater.

10. Serve your gingerbread warm or at room temperature. Place the heavy cream in the small bowl and use the egg beater to whip it until it just forms into peaks. Serve the gingerbread with a spoonful of whipped cream on top of each serving.

PROJECT PAPER ART

In the mid-1800s, professional and amateur artists began experimenting with different art forms. Paper was now mass-produced by machines, which made it plentiful and inexpensive, so it was natural for people to find different ways of using paper. Some copied an art brought to Pennsylvania by settlers from Germany called Pennsylvania Dutch. In this technique, the artist cut the paper into complicated designs. This artform is called *scherenschnitte* (sharon-SCHNIT-a); the word means "scissor cutting." In the 1860s, immigrants from Poland also brought a technique for making beautiful cut paper designs.

In this project, you'll use still another form of paper art, creating a landscape or seascape simply by tearing pieces of colored construction paper. You'll be surprised by the attractive pictures you can create with this technique.

MATERIALS

several sheets of newspaper
several sheets or scraps of construction paper in soft colors, such as blue, gray, pale green, yellow, purple, or brown
piece of lightweight white cardboard or poster board, 8 by 10 inches
scissors
white glue
small dish
water
toothpick
piece of sponge
black felt-tip pen, with fine point

1. Spread several sheets of newspaper over your work surface.

2. Decide whether you want to make a seacoast scene (seascape) or a landscape. Tear 8 or 10 strips of different colors of construction paper. Strips can be from 1 to 4 inches wide and long enough to reach all the way across the 8-by-10-inch cardboard. Make each tear a little unevenly, rather than perfectly straight, to create the curved lines of hills, islands, and the horizon.

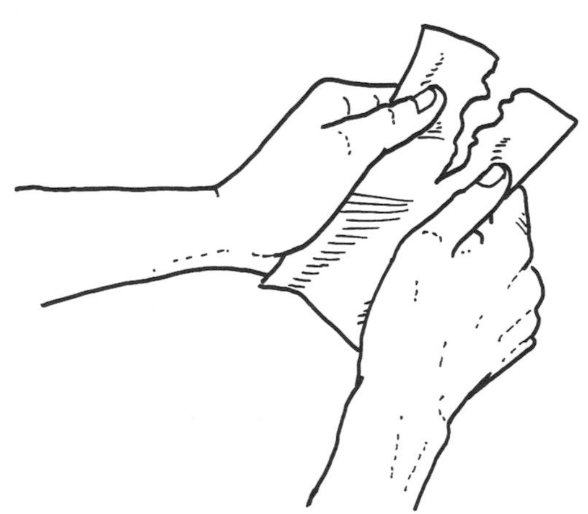

3. Place the cardboard or poster board on your newspaper-covered work surface. Arrange the torn strips in rows across the cardboard to create the image of hills or a seacoast with islands. Cover the entire cardboard surface. The strips can overlap a little, and they can overlap the edges of the cardboard.

4. Decide what you like, or don't like, about the arrangement. Shift strips around to see how your picture changes. Tear additional strips if you need them, or if you want different colors.

5. Look for places to add smaller objects, like a rock, an island, clouds, trees, or a building. Use scissors to cut out these smaller shapes and place them on your landscape or seascape.

6. When you have an arrangement you like, you're ready to glue the pieces onto the backing. Pour some white glue into a small dish and use a toothpick to mix in a little water for easier spreading.

7. Start at the bottom of your picture and glue one piece at a time. Use a damp sponge to cover the back of each piece with a thin coat of glue. Fix the piece in place and go on to the next piece. If any pieces run over the edge of the cardboard backing, trim the overlap with scissors.

8. Allow a few minutes for the glue to dry. Add any details you want with a felt-tip pen. Your paper art is complete.

CHAPTER TWO

SUMMER

- PIGS IN A PEN
- MARZIPAN DECORATIONS
- SHORT'NIN' BREAD
- HOMEMADE CLAY DOUGH SHEEP
- YARN DOLL
- HOPSCOTCH
- MOSAIC PICTURE

The beginning of summer was Emily's favorite time of year because in summer Charleston would be filled with people, parties, concerts, and picnics. Many wealthy plantation families owned summer homes in Charleston. Inland from the coast, where the plantations were located, the summers were hot and humid. To escape the heat, the plantation families moved to Charleston for the summer. It was a season for relaxation and enjoyment.

In 1862, however, the dark clouds of war hung over the small city. A Union army had invaded Virginia, planning to capture Richmond, the capital of the Confederacy. Then, late in the summer, Southerners could finally cheer an important victory. Confederate troops defeated the Union forces near Richmond and forced them to retreat from Virginia.

A SUMMER PARTY

In spite of everyone's worry about the war, Emily enjoyed watching the plantation families open up their summer houses. Her Uncle Ross, Aunt Margaret, and cousin Alexander arrived on schedule. This year, however, there would not be the usual round of picnics at the harbor or lawn parties at people's homes. Instead, the gatherings tended to be quieter visits with friends and relatives.

Some Charleston families had turned their homes into hospitals for men wounded in the war. Emily was delighted when Mama Parkhurst said that she and Alexander could help with a party at one of the hospitals. With Alexander's help, Emily made colorful decorations out of marzipan and baked several recipes of short'nin' bread. The party was a great success because the wounded soldiers enjoyed it so much. Some of the men had fun playing games with Emily and Alexander, including her favorite, called pigs in a pen.

PROJECT PIGS IN A PEN

Americans have always loved games, but in the 1860s some games became amazing fads that swept the country. People wrote entire books and filled magazines with advice and rules about certain games and puzzles. Some of the most popular games needed no more equipment than a sheet of paper and a pencil, like the game called pigs in a pen. The goal of the game is to draw a line that makes the fourth side of a square. The trouble is that your opponent has the same idea.

MATERIALS

sheet of paper
ruler
pencil
2 players

1. On a sheet of paper, use a ruler and pencil to make a grid of dots spaced ½ inch apart. Mark 10 dots in each row. Make sure the rows of dots are exactly parallel to each other, as shown in the diagram.

2. One player goes first by drawing a line connecting any two dots. The line can be up and down, or across, but not diagonal.

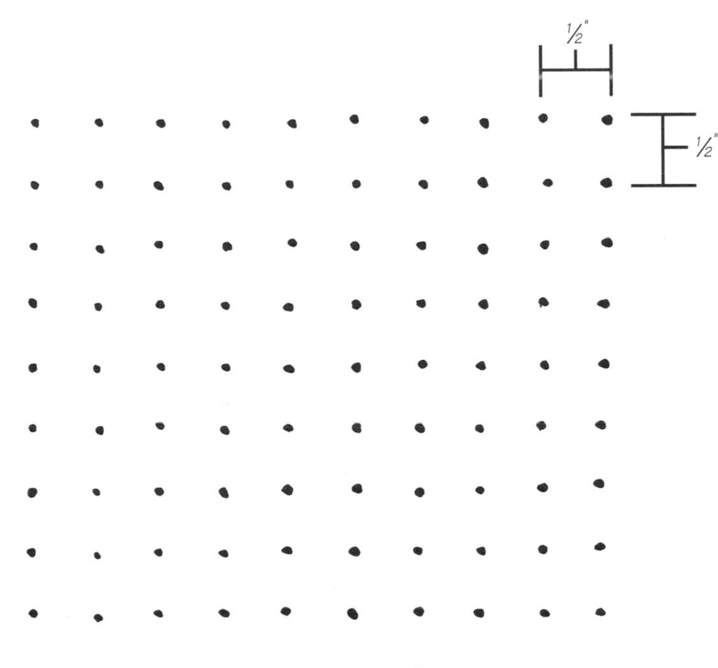

3. The two players take turns, each drawing one line at a time. Each player wants to draw the line that completes a square, meaning that he or she has won that square. For defense, both players try to avoid drawing a line that forms the third side of a square, because the other player will promptly draw the fourth side on her turn. In the beginning, it's easy to avoid drawing a third side. But, as the game sheet is filled in, it becomes harder and harder.

4. Scoring:

(a) When a line is drawn that completes a square, the player writes his or her initial in that square. That means one pig is in the pen.

(b) The player who completes a square gets another turn and draws another line. If that line also completes a square, it is initialed and another line is drawn. The player can keep going as long as each line completes a square.

(c) Players continue taking turns until all dots have been connected. The player who has the most pigs in the pen is the winner.

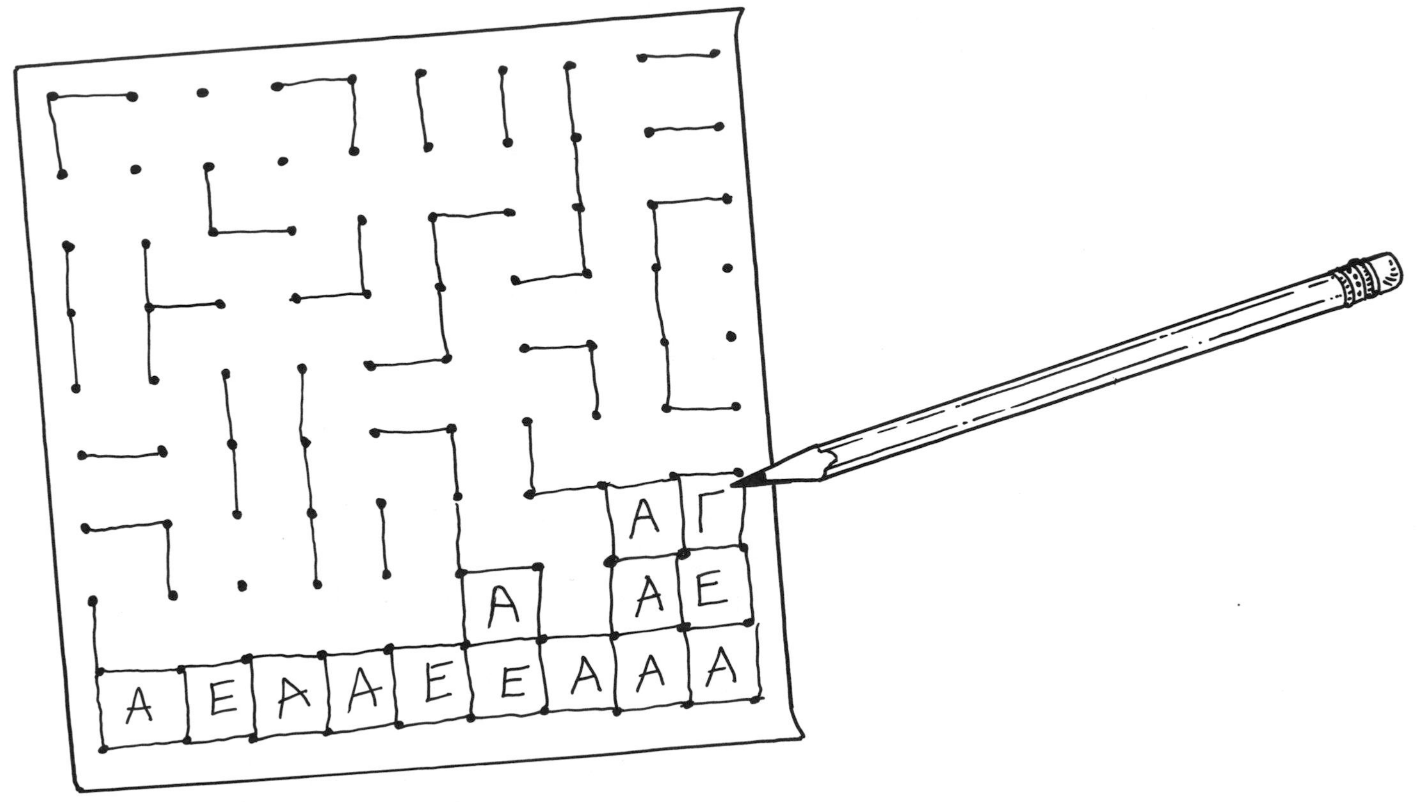

PROJECT MARZIPAN DECORATIONS

Well-to-do families in the South liked to make elaborate decorations for their parties, including miniature fruits, vegetables, and figures made of marzipan. Marzipan is a very sweet substance that is used for pastry fillings as well as for decorations. You'll find it's fun to work with, something like modeling clay you can eat. Use your tiny marzipan sculptures to decorate cupcakes or cakes for special occasions like a birthday party. Wrap any decorations that weren't eaten in a damp cloth and store them in a covered container in the refrigerator. The marzipan will stay fresh for 10 to 12 weeks.

INGREDIENTS

1 8-ounce can or tube of almond paste, available in the baking section of most supermarkets
1¼ cup confectioners' sugar
2 teaspoons almond extract
food coloring: red, yellow, brown, green, orange
tap water
mint leaves, available at most supermarkets (optional)

EQUIPMENT

mixing bowl
bread board or clean countertop
table knife
wax paper
4 or 5 small paper cups or small plates
tweezers (optional)
5 or 6 toothpicks
small paint brush (new or well washed)
wire cooling rack
glass or plastic container with lid

MAKES

about 20 miniature fruits, vegetables, or figures

1. Wash your hands before you begin, then combine the almond paste, 1 cup confectioners' sugar, and the almond extract in a mixing bowl. Mix the ingredients thoroughly with your fingers, then work the mixture into a ball.

2. Sprinkle a little of the leftover sugar onto a bread board or countertop and place the marzipan ball on it.

3. Put a little of the powdered sugar on your fingers and knead the marzipan as though you were working a ball of clay. Continue kneading for 4 or 5 minutes, then press the marzipan flat.

4. With a table knife, cut off a small piece of marzipan, about 1-by-1½ inches. Shape it like clay into whatever tiny form you want—a banana or apple, a flower or leaf, a mouse or a cat. For leaves and stems, use very small pieces of marzipan or real mint leaves and stems. To judge the size of each piece, keep in mind that you have enough marzipan for about 20 figures. Some people like to make very tiny miniatures, while others prefer working with larger shapes, so work with sizes that feel most comfortable to you.

5. When you finish a shape, place it on a sheet of wax paper. Knead the marzipan for a few seconds, then break off another chunk to create a new shape. If the marzipan becomes sticky, work a little powdered sugar into it.

6. After you've made all your marzipan shapes, decide on the colors you need. Shake a few drops of each food coloring into a paper cup or onto a small plate or saucer. Stir in a few drops of water to lighten each color. You can also mix colors, if necessary. Use blue and yellow to make green, for example, or blue and red for purple.

7. To color a piece, you can either dip it into the coloring with tweezers, or paint it with a small brush. Use a toothpick dipped in coloring to add details, like touches of brown on a banana, a bright center on a blossom, or eyes and mouth on a miniature animal.

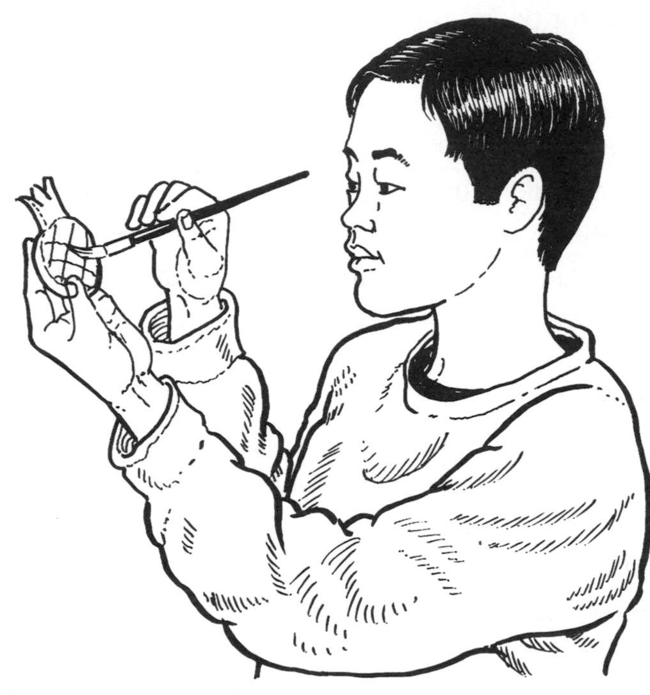

8. Place the finished pieces on a wire cooling rack to dry for 2 to 3 hours. Store them in a covered container until you're ready to use them to decorate a cake, cupcakes, or other dessert. You can also use your marzipan miniatures as party favors, or arrange them on a small plate as a table decoration.

PROJECT SHORT'NIN' BREAD

Scottish immigrants who settled in the South in the 1700s brought a tasty dessert called shortbread to America. Over the years, the Southern name for it changed to shortening bread, or short'nin' bread. It is still called short'nin' bread in much of the South, but shortbread in other parts of the nation. There are several recipes for this crumbly dessert that is half cookie, half cake, and all are delicious. You'll follow one of the oldest and easiest recipes to make short'nin' bread in the shape of a sun, a Scottish symbol for good luck.

INGREDIENTS

1 cup softened butter
½ cup confectioners' sugar
¼ teaspoon salt
½ teaspoon ground cinnamon
2¼ cups all-purpose flour

EQUIPMENT

small saucepan (optional)
large mixing bowl
fork
mixing spoon
cookie sheet
table knife
spatula or pancake flipper
adult helper

Angels of the Battlefield

When the Civil War began, most men believed that caring for the sick and wounded was men's work. They did not think women should be involved in the war in any way. Hundreds of women in both the North and the South ignored this prejudice. In the South, where most of the fighting took place, many women turned their homes into what were called "medical shelters."

In the North, a former teacher named Dorothea Dix persuaded President Lincoln that women could play an important part in nursing the wounded and sick. The president agreed and made her superintendent of nurses for the Union armies. Another former teacher, Clara Barton, took her nursing skills right onto the battlefield and also started a bureau to locate missing soldiers. The soldiers called her the "angel of the battle-field."

MAKES
about 8 dessert servings

1. Allow the butter to soften at room temperature for an hour before you begin, or ask an adult helper to soften it in a small saucepan over low heat.

2. Preheat the oven to 350 degrees F. Wash your hands well before mixing the dough.

3. Place the softened butter in the mixing bowl and stir it vigorously with a fork or mixing spoon to make it creamy.

4. Stir in the sugar, using a fork to mix it well with the butter.

5. Add the salt and cinnamon and stir the mixture well with the fork.

6. Add the flour, a little at a time, stirring with a mixing spoon. When the mixture becomes too thick to stir, continue mixing with your hands. When the flour is completely blended in, don't work the dough any longer. Handling the dough as little as possible makes the short'nin' bread tender and crisp.

7. Shape the dough into a ball and place it on an ungreased cookie sheet. With your hands, press the dough into a flat circle, about ½ inch thick and about 8 inches across.

8. Use a table knife to cut several small triangles out of the edge of the circle, as shown in the picture. This creates your good-luck sun shape.

9. With a fork, prick straight lines across the short'nin' bread to divide it into 8 pie-shaped wedges.

10. Bake the short'nin' bread for 20 to 30 minutes, or until it turns light brown around the edges.

11. Ask your adult helper to remove the cookie sheet from the oven. Cut along the dotted lines with a table knife to make the 8 wedges.

12. Use a pancake flipper or spatula to remove the wedges from the cookie sheet. Serve the short'nin' bread warm or at room temperature.

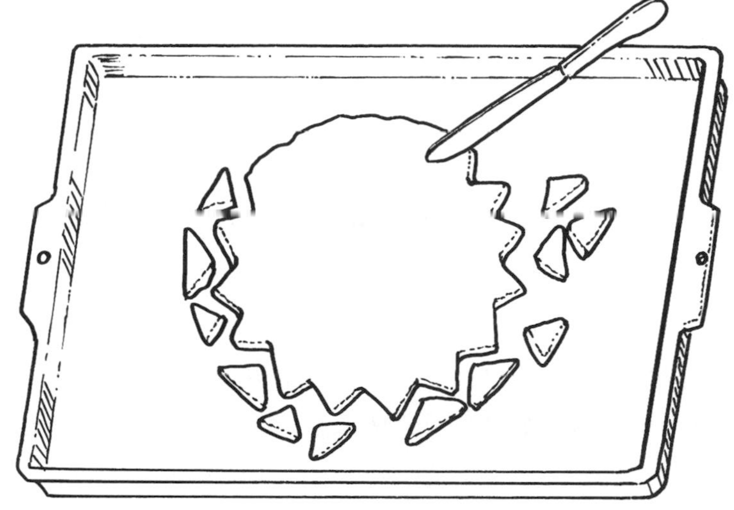

HELPING OUT

By midsummer, the Parkhursts' mill was operating and Emily went almost every day to help. The mill was in the family's warehouse on the waterfront, and was normally used for shipping cotton to the mills in the North and in England. With the harbor now blocked by Union warships, hundreds of bales of cotton were piled on the docks. Sometimes, on the darkest nights, the Parkhursts would send a ship loaded with cotton to try to sneak out of the harbor. Some of the ships made it and delivered their cotton to England, but others were captured by the Union navy.

Inside the mill, about twenty women and a few men worked at turning raw cotton into clothing and other things for the Confederate armies. Farmers had also brought their wool to the mill and workers used that, too. Emily usually worked at a big loom, weaving cotton thread into cloth. In her spare time, she found other things she could do with scraps of fabric, cotton, and yarn. She made a little yarn doll for herself and used fluffy bits of cotton as fleece to cover a small wooden sheep that Alexander carved.

PROJECT HOMEMADE CLAY DOUGH SHEEP

You can buy clay dough in a store, but making your own is a lot more fun; it's easy, and whatever you make hardens like self-hardening clay. The sheep you'll make is like a popular toy of the 1800s—a small pull toy with real fleece covering a sheep carved from wood.

MATERIALS

large saucepan
¾ cup flour
1 teaspoon salad oil
½ cup water
¼ cup salt
1 teaspoon cream of tartar
mixing spoon
several sheets of newspaper
large sheet of wax paper
4½-inch pieces of doweling or sticks
20 to 30 cotton balls
white glue or craft glue
black marking pen
6-inch piece of yarn or ribbon in any bright color
adult helper

1. Place a large saucepan on the stove and measure into it ½ cup of flour, the salad oil, water, salt, and cream of tartar. Stir the mixture well with a mixing spoon.

2. Ask your adult helper to heat the mixture over low to medium heat. Stir constantly. The dough will thicken and slowly form itself into a big lump.

3. When the ball of dough looks like wet clay, turn off the heat and let the dough cool for about 10 minutes.

4. Spread several sheets of newspaper over your work surface and place a large sheet of wax paper on top. Sprinkle the remaining ¼ cup of flour on the wax paper.

5. Place the ball of clay dough on the floured wax paper and knead it like a lump of clay for a minute or two. Shape the clay dough into the body, head, and upper legs of the sheep, as shown in the picture. Add a small piece of clay dough for the tail.

"King Cotton" and Slavery

In 1793, Eli Whitney invented a simple hand-cranked machine called a cotton gin. The gin separated the cotton fibers from its sticky seeds fifty times faster than could be done by hand. With Whitney's invention, cotton suddenly became a much more valuable cash crop—a crop that could be sold for profit. Throughout the South, plantation owners turned more and more land over to growing cotton.

At the same time, other inventions made it possible for mills in New England and in England to produce huge quantities of cotton fabric. The mills could use all the cotton the South could produce.

Cotton became the South's most important product. Throughout the South people said "Cotton is king." But cotton also increased the demand for slaves to work the cotton fields. While every state in the North was ending slavery in the early 1800s, the number of slaves in the South kept growing. When the Civil War began in 1861, one out of every three people in the South was a slave.

6. To complete the legs, push the 4 pieces of dowel or sticks into the clay dough upper legs. About ¼ inch of dowel should show below the clay dough. Adjust these dowel "feet" so your sheep stands firmly.

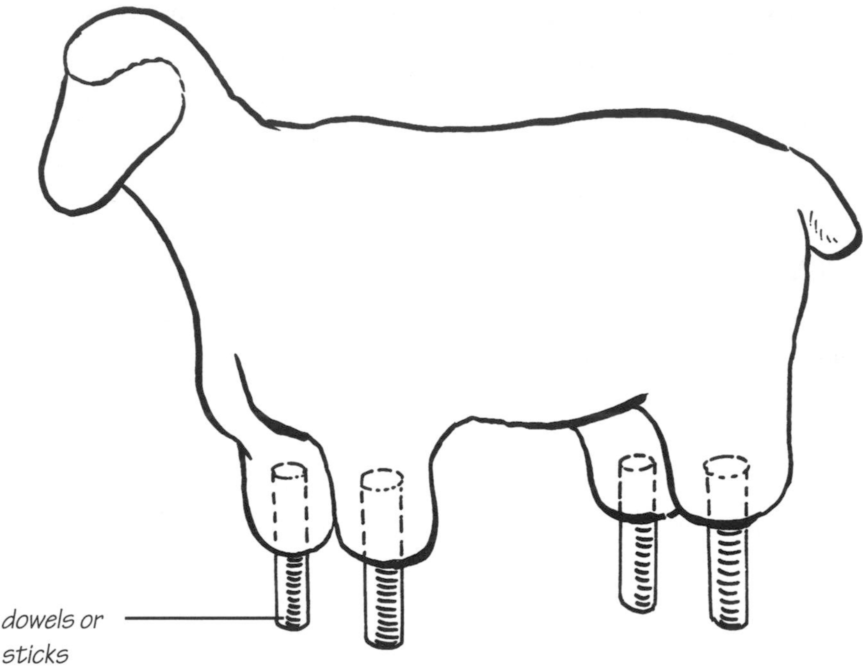

7. Allow your clay dough sheep to harden overnight.

8. Use the marking pen to color the sheep's feet and face.

9. Pull each cotton ball into smaller pieces to look like the fleece on a sheep. Apply a touch of glue to each piece of cotton and glue it on the sheep. Use lots of cotton to make your sheep look fat with fleece. Cover the entire area except for the feet and the face.

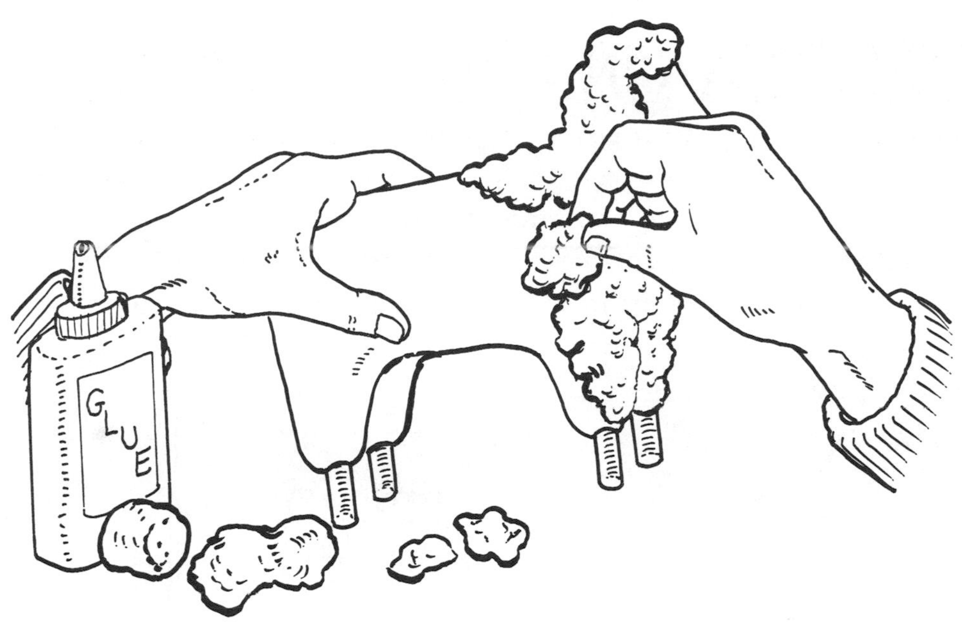

10. For a finishing touch, tie a colorful piece of ribbon or yarn into a bow around the sheep's neck.

YARN DOLL

In the 1860s, people could buy dolls in stores, but many could not afford to buy dolls and most children still liked to make their own dolls. Whether a homemade doll was made from wood, rags, or yarn, each doll was special because it was different from all other dolls. One of the most popular dolls in the 1800s was a simple yarn doll, just like the one you'll make in this project. You can make the doll larger or smaller, if you wish, and you can make it as a girl doll or a boy.

MATERIALS

1 4-ounce skein of yarn, any color (about 6 yards)
scissors
piece of cardboard, about 3 by 6 inches
6 to 10 scraps of yarn, 2 to 3 inches long, blue, black or brown, and red
4 to 5 inches of narrow ribbon, any color
fabric glue, craft glue, or white glue

1. From your skein of yarn, use scissors to cut four pieces 4 inches long and four pieces about 6 inches long. These will be used for tying.

2. Wrap the rest of the skein of yarn around the piece of cardboard the long way. Slide a 6-inch piece of tying yarn under the wrapped yarn and tie it in a firm double knot, as shown in the picture.

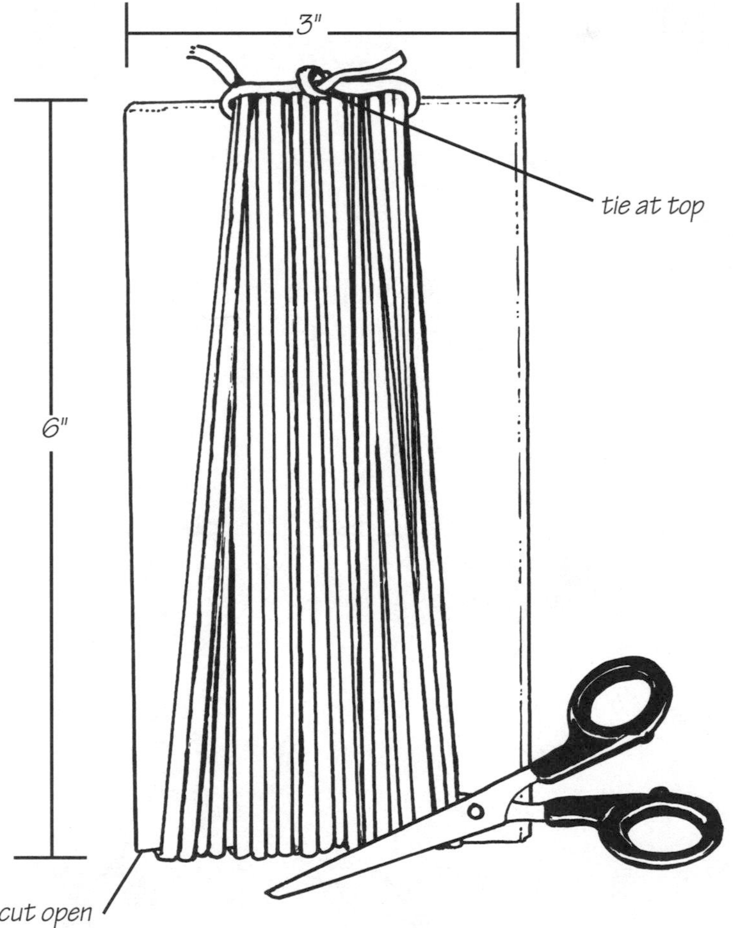

3. At the bottom of the cardboard, cut all the way across the yarn with scissors, as indicated in the drawing. This will remove the yarn from the cardboard.

4. Roll a 6-inch piece of yarn into a ball. Push it into the tied yarn just below the knot. This will help give shape to the doll's head.

5. Below the yarn ball you inserted, tie another 6-inch piece around the yarn to form the doll's neck and head, as shown in the picture.

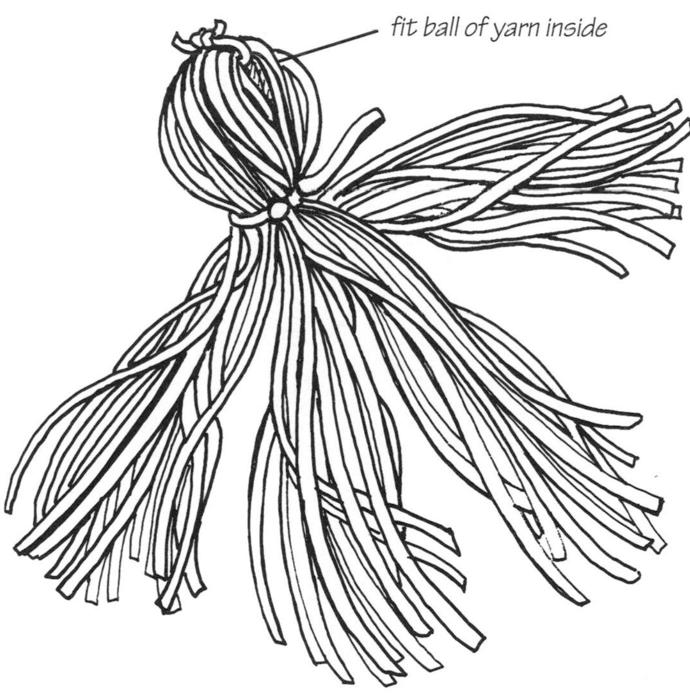

divide into 4 equal sections

6. To form the arms and body, separate the yarn at the bottom into four equal sections. Move the two outer sections away from the rest. These will be the arms. Tie a 4-inch piece of yarn a little more than half way down each of these sections. Tie these wrist pieces in a tight double knot.

7. Cut off the yarn below the wrists, leaving enough yarn to form the doll's hands, as indicated in the picture.

The Golden Age of Doll Making

The years from 1860 to 1890 are often called the golden age of doll making. The fanciest dolls were made in France, not to play with, but to show the latest fashions. When one of these fashion dolls was no longer needed, it might be given to some lucky child.

American and European doll makers were also finding new ways of making dolls for play. Instead of doll heads made of wood or plaster, some doll makers used new materials, including wax and India rubber. Others experimented with walking dolls and dolls with movable heads, arms, and legs, or eyes that opened and closed.

8. Shape the body by tying a 6-inch length of yarn around the waist.

9. To make a boy doll, divide the yarn below the waist into two equal sections. Tie each section at the ankle with a 4-inch piece of yarn. For a girl doll, skip this step.

10. Tuck the ends from all the knots into the doll's body, arms, or legs.

11. For eyes, nose, and buttons, form scraps of different colored yarn into small circles and glue them in place. Use 1 or 2 strands of red yarn for the mouth.

12. For a girl doll's hair, glue 3 or 4 scraps of yarn to the doll's head. Tie the ends of the hair with little ribbon bows to complete your yarn doll.

BACK TO SCHOOL

As the summer drew to a close, Emily and her parents worried that her academy would not open again. Many schools throughout the South had closed because of the war. Most teachers were men, and the men were needed in the Confederate armies. Then, in August, after the Confederate victory near Richmond, the Parkhursts learned that the academy would be open for the 1862–1863 school year.

Emily was delighted that she would soon be in school again, but it meant that she would have less time to spend with her friends and that Alexander would be going back to the plantation. For the final two weeks of the summer, Emily was with Alexander and her two best friends as much as possible. On one rainy afternoon, Grace showed them how to make pictures by pasting seashells on pieces of wood, an art called mosaic. On sunny afternoons, they spent hours playing their favorite outdoor games like hopscotch.

HOPSCOTCH

There are dozens of different ways to play the ancient game of hopscotch, but the object is always the same: to hop on one foot from square to square without stepping on a line, or scotch. You'll play one of the easier versions of the game, a version that was popular in the 1800s. You can have two, three, or four players, and children in the 1800s often played it alone as well.

MATERIALS

sidewalk or other paved surface
piece of chalk
2 to 4 flat stone markers, one for each player
2 to 4 players

1. Use the chalk to mark and number the ten squares on the pavement, as shown in the picture.

2. Flip a coin to decide who goes first. Player 1 tosses his or her marker onto square 1. If the toss misses the correct square, or lands on a line, the turn is over.

3. If the marker lands fairly on square 1, player 1 hops on one foot onto square 2.
Note: A player must never hop onto a square that has a marker on it or the turn is over.

4. Player 1 then hops on the same foot to square 3, and so on, all the way to 10. If, at any time, the player steps on a line, or touches the ground with the other foot, or lands on the wrong square, the turn is over.

5. If player 1 makes it to square 10 without a mistake, he or she hops and turns to face the other way, still on the same foot, then hops back through the squares from 10 to 2. At square 2, player 1 picks up the marker, hops onto square 1, and then hops out of the pattern.

6. A player who goes all the way to 10 and back to 1 can then write his or her chalk initial in any square he or she wishes. In future turns, no other player can land on this square, except that player, who can use that square as a rest stop and stand on it with both feet.

7. When player 1 has finished the pattern, or lost the turn, player 2 goes next by tossing his or her marker onto square 2. Player 2 begins the pattern by hopping from square 1 to square 3, avoiding the square that has the marker.

8. Continue playing the same way, taking turns whenever a player makes a mistake or completes a pattern. With each turn, the players toss the markers farther out, to square 3, then 4, and so on. Players must remember not to hop on a square that has a marker or another player's initial.

9. Winning the game:

The game can end in either of two ways:

(a) When a player tosses his or her marker onto square 10 and then completes the pattern without a mistake.

(b) When the squares are so full of initials that it's impossible to complete the pattern, or if the players run out of time, the player with the most initialed squares is the winner.

Schools in the 1860s

By 1860, most cities in the North offered free public schools, at least for the elementary grades. Public schools in the South and in frontier areas were few in number and widely scattered. Public high schools developed even more slowly. When the Civil War began in 1861, there were fewer than seventy public high schools in the entire country.

There were more than 6,000 private schools, however, where parents paid a tuition fee to send their children. Although the number of schools of all kinds was growing, most Americans received only a few years of schooling. Education was considered of less importance for girls than for boys, although wealthier families usually sent their daughters to high school, and a few young women went on to college.

African Americans had very limited opportunities for education. In the South, it was against the law to teach slaves to read and write. Some free African Americans, however, in both the North and the South, did manage to go to school, usually at private institutions operated by religious groups.

MOSAIC PICTURE

A mosaic is a picture made by gluing or cementing small pieces of material onto a background surface. Mosaics have been made in many parts of the world for nearly 5,000 years, using all sorts of materials, including pebbles, tiles, glass, seashells, cloth, and paper. Floor designs made with colored pieces of tile have been especially popular for hundreds of years. The interest in mosaics declined over several centuries, but they became very popular again in the mid-1800s and are still widely used today.

For your mosaic picture, you'll use different kinds of dried foods, like rice, cream of wheat, and split peas. You can either copy the picture of "the owl and the pussycat," or make your own drawing, such as a simple scene, a real or make-believe animal, or a design. Use the dried foods listed, or try others you find at home, like coffee beans, lentils, macaroni, or seeds. Once you've had the fun of making a mosaic, try one with other materials, such as pebbles or seashells. You can also use mosaics to cover any box that has a stiff surface.

MATERIALS

several sheets of newspaper
piece of stiff cardboard, masonite, or plywood, 3½ by 7 inches
pencil
ruler
piece of gray construction paper, 3½ by 7 inches
piece of blue construction paper, about 2 by 7 inches
scissors
white glue
craft stick or other stick for stirring
piece of sponge

6 tablespoons of dried split peas
6 to 8 tablespoons each of ground coffee, brown rice, and cream of wheat
3 to 5 small paper cups
6 cloves or peppercorns
2 to 4 pieces of uncooked spaghetti
tweezers or toothpick
damp rag or paper towel
can of hair spray (optional)

1. Spread several sheets of newspaper over your work surface. Place the cardboard or other backing material on top.

2. Spread white glue on the back of the gray construction paper "sea" and glue it to the cardboard. *Tip: The glue will spread more easily if you add a little water. Use the stick to mix in the water. Use a piece of damp sponge to spread the glue evenly.*

3. Cut the blue construction paper "sky" to fill the top part of your picture, about 1½ by 7 inches. It's okay for the construction paper pieces to overlap a little. Glue the sky in place and allow the glue to dry for 10 to 15 minutes.

4. Copy the outline of the picture in pencil on the construction paper. If you create your own picture or design, keep it simple—a few large forms or shapes and very little detail.

5. Measure the ground coffee, brown rice, and cream of wheat into the small paper cups. Put the cloves or peppercorns in a paper cup, or simply set them on a corner of your work surface with the spaghetti. (If the spaghetti is very thin, use 4 pieces.)

6. To apply your mosaic materials, start at the top of the picture and work toward the bottom. Carefully spread a coat of glue on one cloud and sprinkle about half the cream of wheat on the wet glue. Repeat with the other cloud.

7. Spread a thin coat of glue on one piece of spaghetti and position it on the picture for the mast. Break the second piece of spaghetti in two and place them on the picture as the cross-tree for the mast.
Tips: You'll find it helpful to use tweezers or a toothpick to move pieces into exactly the position you want. Keep a damp rag or paper towel handy for wiping your fingers if they become sticky.

8. Apply the brown rice on the owl and the ground coffee on the pussycat the same way you made the clouds in step 6.

9. Use the round part of the cloves (or peppercorns) for the eyes of both and for the cat's nose.

Use the stem of a clove for the owl's beak. Hold each piece in your fingers, or with tweezers, apply a dab of glue, and position the piece on the picture.

10. Follow step 6 to apply the split peas for the boat. Let the glue dry for about 10 minutes, then tip the picture and tap it lightly so that any loose material falls onto the newspaper. Fill in any gaps in the boat by applying individual pieces to the picture.

11. To make your mosaic last longer, you can use hair spray in a well-ventilated area. Hold the can about 8 inches from the picture and spray on a thin coat with a quick back and forth motion. Let the spray dry for a minute or two, then apply a second coat. Use very little spray or it will run and damage the picture. Prop your completed mosaic on a bookcase or dresser.

CHAPTER THREE

AKWABA DOLL ORNAMENT

JARABADASH: A GAME OF STRATEGY

MORSE CODE MESSAGES

MODEL FORT SUMTER FLAG

DRIED APPLE RINGS

PINE CONE TURKEY

PUMPKIN PIE

Far to the north of Charleston, the Wheeler family and several friends gathered in the Wheelers' small New York City apartment. Everyone was excited by the day's news that President Abraham Lincoln had issued his Emancipation Proclamation. As of January 1, 1863, the president declared, all slaves in the states still fighting the Union would be officially free. Pa Wheeler explained that none of the slaves were actually free yet. The North would have to win the war to set them free. For millions of people, however, white as well as African American, the proclamation meant that the North was now fighting to free the slaves as well as to restore the nation's unity.

Solomon Wheeler also told the family and friends that the Union armies would now allow men of African descent to enlist and that he planned to join up. Tim was proud that Pa would be fighting for the Union.

AFRICAN HERITAGE

Both of Tim's parents had been born in America, but his Grandma Esther had been a young girl in western Africa when her entire family was kidnapped and sold into slavery. Tim loved listening to her describe what it was like growing up in Africa.

Almost every evening that autumn, Grandma Esther told Tim and little Lisa wonderful stories about life in the Ashanti kingdom where she had lived. Some stories were about Anansi the spider, who always outsmarted his bigger and stronger enemies. Grandma taught Tim and his ten-year-old friend Rachel how to play games like *jarabadash* and how to make good-luck charms called *akwaba* dolls.

PROJECT *AKWABA* DOLL ORNAMENT

Among the Ashanti people of western Africa, girls and young women carried small *akwaba* dolls as both ornaments and good-luck charms. They tucked the wood or clay carvings into their garments or wore them on strings around their necks. The unusual shapes of the dolls had special meanings. The arms, head, and body formed a cross, called the cross of life. The dolls were also meant to bring the wearer a healthy baby when she was grown up and married. A square or rectangular head meant that the baby would be a boy, an oval head meant a girl child, and a perfectly round head was for a wise child who would become a leader.

You'll make your *akwaba* doll out of self-hardening clay, or your own homemade clay dough, following the directions in the clay dough sheep project on page 37. Carry the doll in your pocket, or hang it on a belt as a good-luck charm, or make several to use as ornaments for a Christmas tree or Kwanza celebration, or simply as decorations for your room.

MATERIALS

several sheets of newspaper
sheet of wax paper
¼ pound self-hardening clay, available in craft and hobby sections of most discount department stores, or your own homemade clay dough
rolling pin or round glass jar
pencil
craft stick or table knife
large nail
blue, black, and red marking pens
6-inch piece of yarn, any color

1. Spread several sheets of newspaper on your work surface and place a sheet of wax paper on top. (The wax paper will keep the newsprint from discoloring the clay.)

2. If you're using self-hardening clay, follow the instructions on the package for kneading the clay to make it soft and easy to form.

3. Place the clay or clay dough on the wax paper. Use a rolling pin or a sturdy glass jar to roll the clay flat, ¼ to ⅓ inch thick.

4. Decide whether your *akwaba* doll will represent a boy, a girl, or a wise one. Use a pencil to draw the outline of the figure on the clay. Make the head about ⅓ of the total length. You can make the figure from head to foot as small as 2 inches or as large as 3½ inches.

5. Cut out the figure with a craft stick or table knife, and use a nail to make a hole near the top of the head for stringing. Let the figure harden overnight, or follow the directions on the package of self-hardening clay.

6. When the figure is hard, draw a design in pencil on it, including facial features. Use one of the designs shown in the picture or create your own. Color the face and design with marking pens, using any color scheme you wish.

7. Run the piece of yarn through the hole and tie the ends in a firm double knot. Your *akwaba* doll is ready to bring good luck.

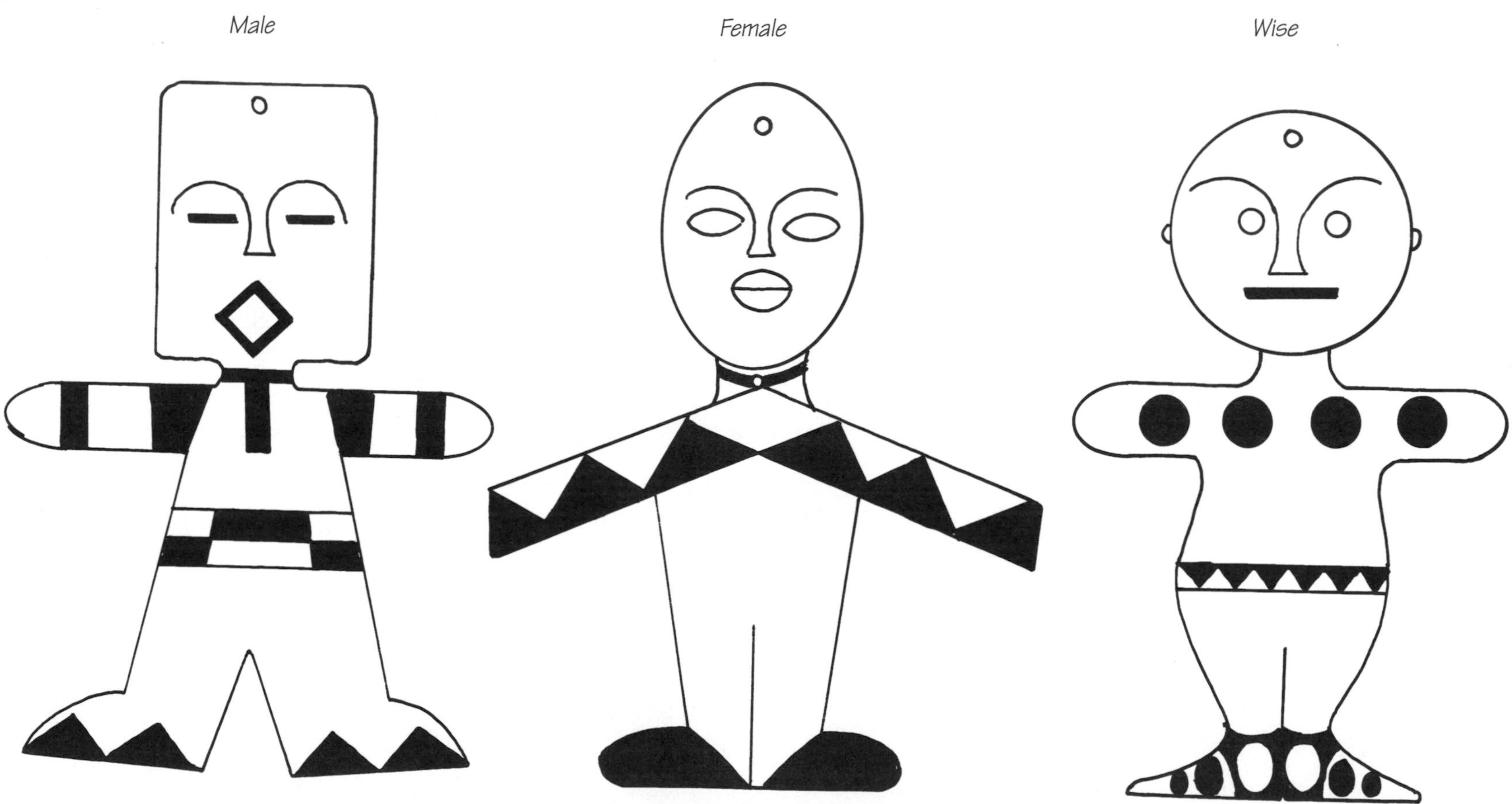

PROJECT *JARABADASH:* A GAME OF STRATEGY

In the villages of western Africa, *jarabadash* is played in the dirt, using small stones as game pieces. The game is similar to tic-tac-toe—the goal for each player is to place three markers in a row without being blocked. And, like tic-tac-toe, the row of three can be a diagonal line through the center. But *jarabadash* is really more difficult. Once all six markers have been placed, players take turns moving one space at a time, each trying to make a row of three. The player with the best strategy will win.

MATERIALS

sheet of paper
ruler
pencil
scrap of cardboard or white poster board
scissors
black felt-tip marker
2 players

1. Divide the sheet of paper into four 4-inch squares, as shown in the diagram.

2. With a pencil, mark off and number the nine positions on the game sheet.

3. With scissors, cut a piece of cardboard or poster board into six oval game pieces, each about ¼ inch long. Color three of the game pieces black with the felt-tip pen. One player will have three white markers, the other has the three black ones.

African American Contributions to Music

Although the slaves who were brought to America were completely cut off from their African homelands, they kept alive many of their cultural traditions, such as crafts, religious ceremonies, dance, and music. In music, slaves and free African Americans combined African sounds and rhythms to create new forms. In religious music, for example, people of African descent retold Bible stories in songs called spirituals, or Gospel music. After the Civil War, groups of Gospel singers began touring the United States, Canada, and Europe, and the popularity of Gospel music continues today.

The heritage of African rhythms and melodies led to other new musical forms. In the late 1800s, African American musicians in the South produced music known as "the blues," and composer Scott Joplin created a musical style called "ragtime." Early in the 1900s, other African Americans in New Orleans and other cities developed still another famous musical form—jazz.

African American Soldiers and Sailors

Until President Lincoln issued the Emancipation Proclamation in September 1862, African Americans were not accepted in the Union armies. Some Union generals, however, formed volunteer units without authority, especially in areas of the South occupied by Union forces. With the president's proclamation, enlistments of men of African descent were permitted, and thousands rushed to sign up.

An estimated 186,000 African Americans served in the armies of the North, and another 30,000 in the navy. Although these volunteers were segregated (separated) into "colored regiments" with white officers, they were proud to be fighting for their country and for freedom. African American soldiers took part in thirty-nine major battles, and sixteen men received the Congressional Medal of Honor, the highest award for bravery.

4. Rules for *jarabadash:*

(a) Just as in tic-tac-toe, the two players take turns, placing one marker at a time. Each player tries to place three markers in a row (including the diagonal, or through the center), and also tries to block the other player.

(b) After all six markers have been placed, the players continue to take turns, moving one marker one position at a time. These moves must be along the lines, not on the diagonal.

On the sample board, for example, white will place her marker on position 5 to block black's diagonal row. This puts black in a tough spot. He has to get a marker to position 3 to block white, but he can only move one position on his turn. White will win the game.

(c) Play continues until one player makes a row of three, or until both players are blocked, creating a tie.

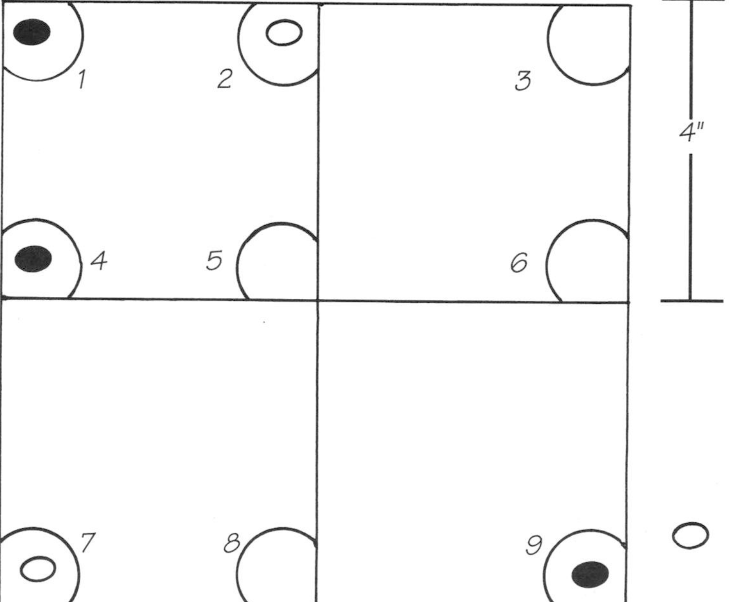

JOINING THE FIGHT FOR FREEDOM

When Solomon Wheeler learned that one of the first African American regiments was being organized in Boston, Hannah agreed that he should go there to enlist. On a crisp autumn morning, the family proudly watched Solomon board a ship for the voyage to Boston. Although they worried about his safety, they also hoped that he would soon be a volunteer in the 54th Massachusetts Regiment.

With Pa away, Tim took a job as a newsboy to help make up for Pa's lost wages. Every afternoon after school, he sold his newspapers on a busy street corner, then took his earnings home to Ma. It gave him a good feeling to be contributing to the family's welfare.

Tim and his friend Rachel also began exploring things related to the war. They read newspaper accounts of battles, and they started a scrapbook with the drawings and photographs printed in the papers. They made a model military flag for Pa's regiment. And, since the Union armies used the telegraph to send messages, they practiced sending messages to each other in Morse Code.

PROJECT MORSE CODE MESSAGES

In Civil War days, the fastest way to send messages was by telegraph. By the early 1860s, telegraph wires connected all the cities and towns east of the Mississippi River, and lines were also stretching westward. A telegraph operator tapped out the dot-and-dash messages in Morse Code. The short and long taps were carried over the telegraph wires as short and long electrical impulses to the receiving end, where another telegrapher wrote out the message. A message could be transmitted hundreds of miles in a matter of seconds. Ships at sea used lanterns to flash messages in the same code.

With a friend, you can try tapping out Morse Code messages to each other, but you'll probably find that flashlight signals are easier to send and receive. You'll also discover why people kept their telegrams short and simple.

MATERIALS

2 pencils
2 sheets of paper or note pads
2 flashlights
partner

1. A good way to get used to working with Morse Code is to write out the dots and dashes of a simple message. Try writing a few words in code to your partner while he or she writes one to you. In a brief message like this, it isn't necessary to include codes for beginning and ending the transmission, or even the code for the question mark. Here's a sample:

···· · ·_·· ·_·· _ _ _ ·_·_·_ ·_ _ ···· ·_ _ ··· _· · ·_ _

Hello (period) Whats new

2. Exchange your messages and decode them. It probably seems very slow to you, but if you were sending a message several hundred miles in the 1860s, it would be remarkably speedy. Also, expert telegraphers could tap the keys with lightning speed.

3. Now try tapping out a message to your partner simply by tapping your pencil on a hard surface. Your partner will try to write down the dots and dashes. You'll find this is a lot more difficult because it's hard to distinguish dashes from the space between letters. Try it a few times and see if your transmission and receiving become more accurate.

4. Write out the code for new messages to each other. Use a flashlight to flash long and short signals to your partner, while he or she writes them down. Then your partner flashes the new message to you. Write down the code you receive, then transcribe it into words. The flash-light dots and dashes should work best because they're most similar to the electrical impulses of a real telegraph.

5. Once you're comfortable with Morse Code, try sending flashlight messages for your partner to answer in code.

MORSE CODE

A ·—	N —·	1 ·————
B —···	O ———	2 ··———
C —·—·	P ·——·	3 ···——
D —··	Q ——·—	4 ····—
E ·	R ·—·	5 ·····
F ··—·	S ···	6 —····
G ——·	T —	7 ——···
H ····	U ··—	8 ———··
I ··	V ···—	9 ————·
J ·———	W ·——	0 —————
K —·—	X —··—	
L ·—··	Y —·——	
M ——	Z ——··	

Beginning of transmission —·—·—
Error ········
End of transmission ·—·—·
period ·— ·— ·—
comma ——·· ——
question ·· —— ··

Samuel F. B. Morse and the Telegraph

In the 1830s, inventors in the United States and Europe were trying to develop a telegraph system, but Samuel F .B. Morse perfected the first, including the dot-dash code that is still known by his name.

The telegraph created a revolution in communication. Until Morse, messages could be sent only by horseback or sailing ship. With the telegraph, a message could be sent almost as fast as the telegrapher could tap the keys.

Morse became wealthy from his invention and gave most of his fortune to worthy causes, including a new college for women. During the Civil War, incidentally, one of the fastest of the hundreds of telegraphers was a young man named Thomas Alva Edison.

MODEL FORT SUMTER FLAG

In this project, you'll make a model of the famous Fort Sumter flag, including the tatters and holes from the first shots of the Civil War. The best fabric for gluing is normally felt because it doesn't ravel. In this activity, however, you'll use cotton so that it will ravel to create the ragged look of the real flag. (Almost 40,000 cannon shots were exchanged the day of the battle, and several shell fragments tore through the flag.) You can buy fabric remnants in most discount department stores or fabric stores.

MATERIALS

several sheets of newspaper
white cotton fabric, about 14 by 24 inches, or an old dish towel
ruler
pencil
scissors
dark blue cotton fabric, 6 by 7 inches
fabric glue or white glue
red cotton fabric, about 10 by 20 inches needed
piece of scrap cardboard

1. Spread several sheets of newspaper on your work surface and place the white fabric on top.

2. With ruler and pencil, mark the dimensions for your model flag on the fabric—13 by 19 inches. Cut the fabric along those lines with scissors. Save the leftover cloth.

3. Spread very thin spots of glue on one side of the blue cloth. (If the glue is too thick, it will show through the fabric.) Position the blue rectangle in the upper left corner of the white fabric with the 6-inch side along the top of the flag, as indicated in the picture. Press the blue cloth in place.

4. Cut four strips of the red fabric 1 inch wide and 13 inches long. Position the four strips on the upper part of the flag. As you can see in the picture, the bottom edge of one red strip matches the bottom edge of the blue rectangle. When you have the four strips lined up correctly, glue them to the white fabric, starting with the top strip.

5. Cut three more strips of red fabric, 1 inch wide and 19 inches long. Position them on the lower part of the flag, then glue them in place.

6. On a piece of cardboard, copy the drawing of the star in pencil. Cut out the star and use it as a pattern to make a total of 33 stars, representing the number of states in 1861.

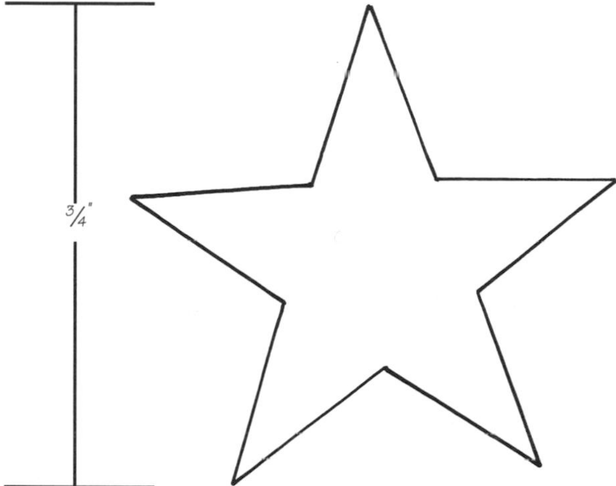

7. Notice the positioning of the stars on the flag in the picture on page 60. Start in the center of the blue rectangle and glue the column of seven stars to the blue background. Work out from this center column in both directions until all 33 stars are glued in place.

8. Use scissors to cut jagged edges along the top, bottom, and right side of the flag. There is no special pattern to follow—you simply want the flag to look tattered. You can add the frayed look by pulling some of the loose threads.

9. Poke the point of the scissors through the flag in several places, as shown in the picture. Cut jagged holes in the flag and pull some of the loose threads. Here, too, there is no special pattern to follow; that is, the holes don't have to be in the exact location of the flag in the picture.

The Fort Sumter Flag

Fort Sumter, in Charleston Harbor, was still held by Union troops in April 1861. Then, on the morning of April 12, Confederate cannons in Charleston opened fire on the fort. Those were the opening shots of the Civil War.

The Union soldiers in Fort Sumter were forced to surrender the next day. Confederate troops occupied the fort, lowered the tattered American flag, and raised the flag of the Confederacy. The fort remained in Southern hands until the end of the war.

After the war, the original torn flag became an important symbol of the courage and dedication of the men and women on both sides in this tragic war.

10. If any of the stars or stripes have worked loose with the cutting, glue them back in place. Your model Fort Sumter flag is now ready to pin or tack to the wall of your room.

Note: Cutting the flag in this way is not considered a desecration of the flag, especially since you are doing it to honor a particular historical flag.

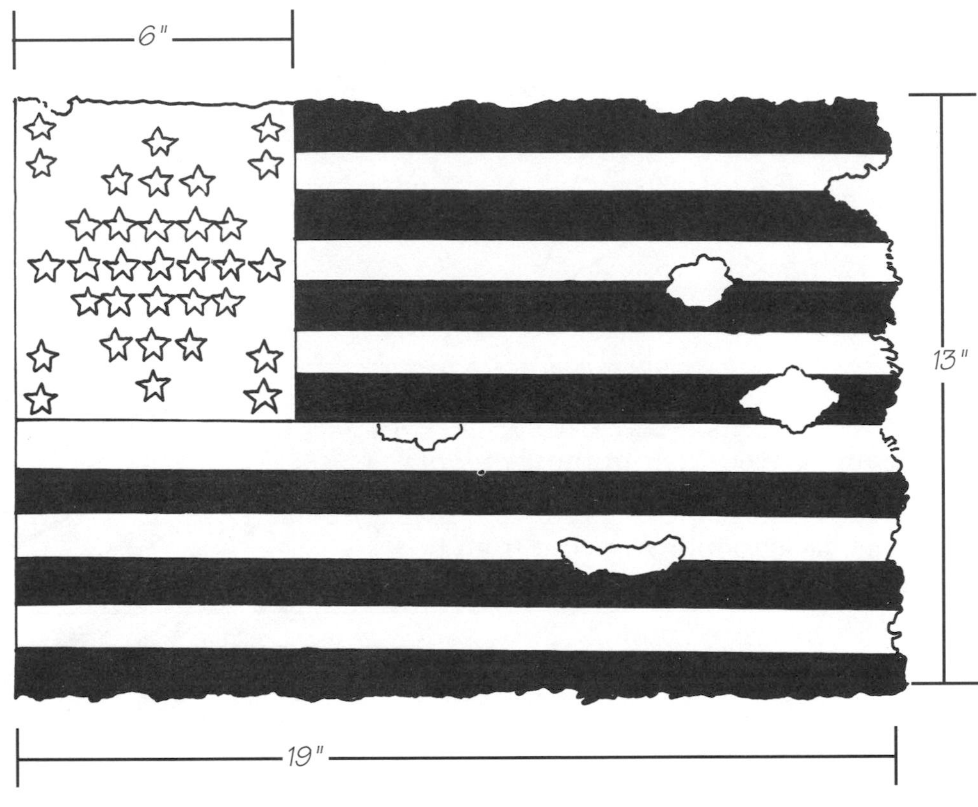

TIM IN THE KITCHEN

Hannah Wheeler worked long hours in the general store, and she was grateful that Tim and Grandma Esther could look after Lisa and prepare meals. In mid-November, however, Grandma Esther slipped on a patch of ice and suffered a badly sprained ankle. It would be weeks before she could walk, so cooking the evening meal presented a serious problem. Tim managed to convince his mother that he could do the cooking with Grandma giving him directions.

For Tim, the biggest challenge was preparing the Thanksgiving Day meal. His friend Rachel helped, Lisa did what she could, and Grandma Esther gave step-by-step instructions. Rachel made miniature turkeys out of pine cones for decorations. She and her parents and two younger brothers joined the Wheelers for the Thanksgiving feast. Tim and Rachel proudly served the meal, topped off with Tim's first pumpkin pie for dessert. Although the kitchen was a mess, everyone agreed that the feast was a great success. Tim enjoyed his kitchen duties, especially chores that were fun, like making dried apple rings, but he felt relieved when Grandma Esther could finally take over again.

DRIED APPLE RINGS

Throughout the 1700s and 1800s, Americans used a variety of methods to preserve apples from each year's autumn harvest. Drying apple rings on wooden racks or on strings was one of the easiest and simplest techniques. Apple rings make a chewy and nutritious snack, or you can use some as a tasty topping on hot breakfast cereal. For the best dried rings, use firm, tart apples, such as Baldwins, Romes, Winesaps, or Ida Reds.

INGREDIENTS

¼ cup lemon juice
tap water
3 or 4 fresh apples

EQUIPMENT

mixing bowl
paring knife, or fruit parer and corer, to be used by adult helper
3 to 4 feet of string or twine
large piece of cheesecloth (optional)
large glass or plastic container with lid
adult helper

MAKES

about 12 snack servings

1. Measure the lemon juice into the mixing bowl and fill the bowl half way with cold tap water.

2. Have your adult helper peel and core the apples, then slice them into rings about ¼ inch thick. As each apple is sliced, quickly place the rings in the bowl of lemon water. This will keep the apples from turning brown.

3. Run the string or twine through the rings. Tie the ends of the strings between two chairs or other suitable objects in a warm, dry location with good air circulation. A clean basement near a furnace is ideal, or you can even hang the string in your room, especially near a heater. On bright, sunny days, you can hang the string outdoors, covered with cheesecloth, to speed the drying, but you have to bring it in at night or during wet weather. Indoor drying takes 2 to 3 weeks (instead of 1 week outdoors), but it is a less troublesome method.

4. After two weeks, remove one of the rings and test it by taking a bite. It should be quite chewy and dry all the way through. When the rings are completely dried, remove them from the string. Try some for a snack, or on cereal, and store the rest in a covered jar. The dried apple rings will remain unspoiled for at least 2 to 3 months.

PINE CONE TURKEY

In the 1800s, most Americans made their own holiday decorations. They often made use of whatever materials they found in their surroundings—for example, during the Christmas season they would use evergreen boughs, pine cones, and holly. For autumn celebrations, they used symbols of the harvest, such as sheaves of wheat, corn, and Indian corn, and figures made of straw. In the tradition of handmade decorations, you'll make a turkey ornament out of a pine cone, a pipe cleaner, and construction paper. If you can't find a pine cone near your home, ask at any florist shop or hobby and craft store. Use your turkey as a table decoration, or make several to hang as a mobile.

MATERIALS

several sheets of newspaper
1 pipe cleaner
brown poster paint or acrylic paint
small paintbrush
scraps of construction paper, in 3 to 5 colors, including red
ruler
pencil
scissors
pine cone, any size, but plump rather than long and thin
white glue
red marking pen or felt-tip pen (optional)
large pin, such as a corsage pin or map pin, but any large pin will do
10 to 12 inches black thread (optional)

1. Spread several sheets of newspaper on your work surface.

2. Use a small paintbrush and a little acrylic paint or poster paint to color the pipe cleaner brown. Set the pipe cleaner aside to dry for 10 to 15 minutes.

3. While the paint dries, use a pencil to copy the model of a wing on colored construction paper. For a colorful decoration, use a variety of colors for the wings and feathers, rather than the turkey's natural coloring. Cut out the construction paper wing with scissors and use it as a pattern to draw and cut out a second wing.

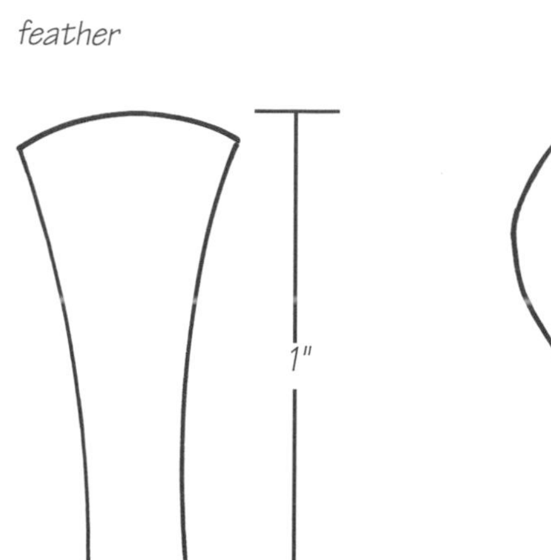

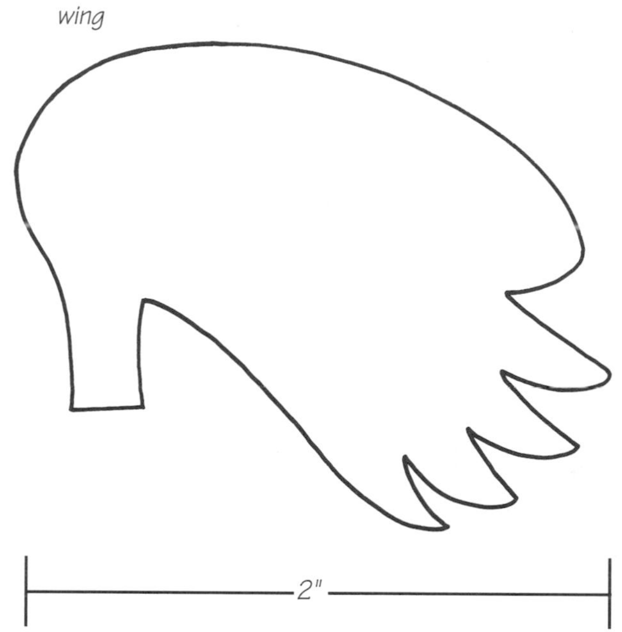

4. Use the same technique to make 12 to 14 feathers in different colors. If your pine cone is large, cut 4 or 5 additional feathers.

5. When the paint on the pipe cleaner is dry, bend one end into a tight circle, forming the turkey's head and eye, as shown in the picture. Leave a small end piece sticking out for the beak.

6. Place the pine cone on the newspaper and hold the pipe cleaner near the stem of the cone. Decide how long the turkey's neck should be and cut off the extra part of the pipe cleaner.

Thanksgiving Day Becomes Official

The first Thanksgiving celebration in America was held by the Pilgrims at Plymouth Bay in December 1621. After surviving a hard beginning in their little colony, the Pilgrims followed a European tradition of thanking God for a bountiful harvest. They also invited ninety of the Native Americans who had helped them survive their first difficult year. The celebration and feasting lasted nearly a week.

In the years that followed Americans continued to celebrate Thanksgiving, but the date and the way of celebrating depended on local customs. In 1789, President George Washington called for a nationwide day of Thanksgiving to give thanks for the new Constitution of the United States. Then, during the Civil War, President Abraham Lincoln proclaimed that Thanksgiving would be a national holiday. It would be celebrated every year on the last Thursday in November, beginning in 1863. Later, in 1941, Congress changed the day to the fourth Thursday in November.

7. Put a little white glue on the base of the pipe cleaner neck and push it into the pine cone in between petals.

8. Cut a small piece of red construction paper for the turkey's wattle. Glue this piece just below the beak, almost like a beard. (If you don't have red construction paper, use a red marking pen or felt-tip pen to color a piece of paper.)

9. Put a little glue on the stems of the tail feathers, one at a time, and push them in between the pine cone petals. Make two rows of feathers in a fan shape, as shown.

10. Repeat step 9 to attach a wing to either side of the cone.

11. Stick a large pin into the top of the back, as indicated in the picture. This provides an easy way to move your pine cone turkey from place to place. If you want to hang the decoration, or use it in a mobile, tie a piece of black thread to the top of the pin.

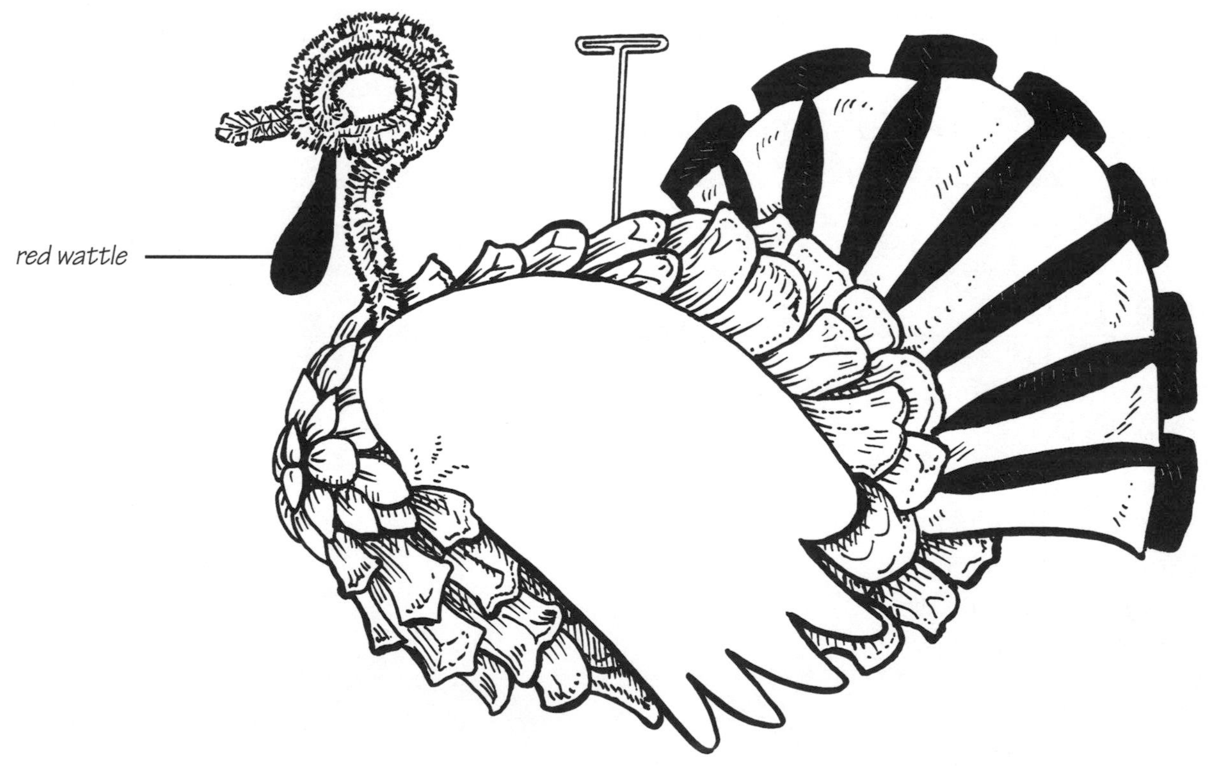

PROJECT PUMPKIN PIE

Pumpkin pie has been part of the traditional Thanksgiving Day feast for more than 150 years. In the 1800s, people made the pie from scratch. They cut the pumpkin into chunks, peeled off the skin, and removed the seeds. They then cooked the pumpkin meat, pushed it through a strainer, and placed it in their homemade piecrust. Some people still prefer the traditional method, but you'll follow a simpler modern recipe using canned pumpkin and a ready-made pie shell. The seasonings you add, however, are the same as those used in the 1800s.

INGREDIENTS

¾ cup sugar
¼ teaspoon salt
2 teaspoons ground cinnamon
½ teaspoon ground ginger
¼ teaspoon ground cloves
2 eggs
1 15-ounce can pumpkin (1¾ cups)
1 12-ounce can evaporated milk (1½ cups)
1 9-inch unbaked pie shell
1 cup whipping cream

EQUIPMENT

small mixing bowl
mixing spoon
large mixing bowl
egg beater
aluminum baking sheet (optional)
table knife
wire cooling rack
adult helper

MAKES

6 to 8 servings

1. Preheat the oven to 400 degrees F.

2. Measure the sugar, salt, cinnamon, ginger, and cloves into the small mixing bowl. Stir with a mixing spoon to blend the ingredients.

3. Break the eggs into the large mixing bowl. Beat them with the egg beater for about two minutes.

4. Add the pumpkin to the eggs and stir well.

5. Pour the sugar-spice mixture into the large bowl with the pumpkin and eggs. Stir well to mix all the ingredients.

Condensed Milk and Canned Foods

In the early 1800s, inventors in France and England had developed ways to preserve food in tin cans, but the technique was slow to catch on in America. The Civil War and the work of a man named Gail Borden helped to make canned foods popular.

Borden invented a way to condense milk by evaporating most of the water. He found that one quart of his condensed milk made 5 or 6 quarts of regular milk when water was added. In addition, the sealed tin cans kept the condensed milk fresh for months. Borden started a condensed milk company in 1857 and was fairly successful. Then, when the Civil War began, people discovered that the small, lightweight cans of Borden's milk were perfect for soldiers' rations. Since the company was located in the North, the Union army became Borden's best customer. The popularity of condensed milk with the soldiers helped convince the public that all canned foods were safe and convenient. By 1870, Americans were buying 30 million cans of food and milk every year.

6. Slowly pour in the evaporated milk, stirring constantly. Continue stirring until all the ingredients are blended.

7. Pour the mixture into the pie shell and bake for 15 minutes. *Note: If the pie pan is made of foil or metal, place a baking sheet under it so that the crust bakes properly.*

8. After 15 minutes, turn the oven down to 350 degrees and continue baking for 45 to 50 minutes. To test the pie, insert a table knife near the center of the pie; when the knife comes out clean, the pie is done.

9. Ask your adult helper to remove the pie from the oven. Place it on a wire cooling rack.

10. Before serving, use an egg beater to whip the cream until it forms peaks. Top each piece of pie with a small mound of whipped cream and serve.

CHAPTER FOUR

- FLOATING BALL
- GAME OF *MANKALA*
- EVERGREEN WREATH
- POTATO-PRINT WRAPPING PAPER
- APPLE PANDOWDY DESSERT
- REVOLVING SERPENT
- TUMBLING PUPPIES

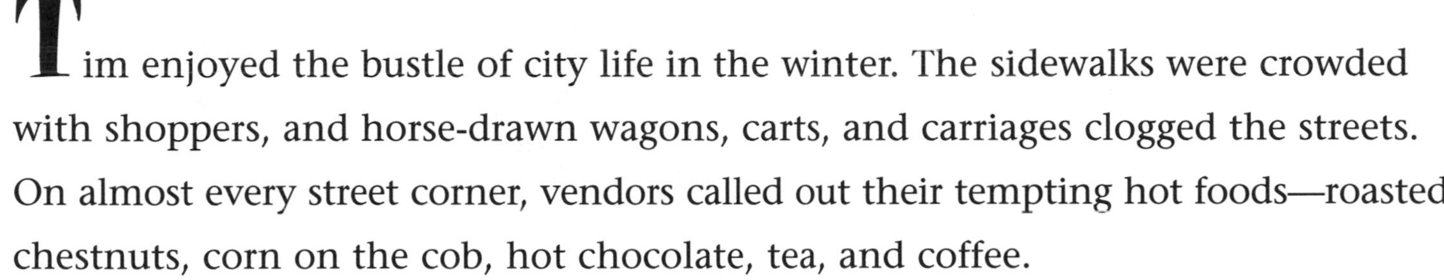

Tim enjoyed the bustle of city life in the winter. The sidewalks were crowded with shoppers, and horse-drawn wagons, carts, and carriages clogged the streets. On almost every street corner, vendors called out their tempting hot foods—roasted chestnuts, corn on the cob, hot chocolate, tea, and coffee.

Sometimes, on the docks where Pa worked, Tim would watch a shipload of immigrants from Europe coming on shore. Even though the nation was torn by war, thousands of these newcomers continued to arrive every month, seeking freedom from harsh governments, jobs in the factories and mills, or land to farm on the western frontier.

When Tim finished selling his newspapers, he always stopped in the general store to see Ma. Then he climbed the two flights of stairs to their three-room apartment, where Grandma Esther and Lisa were preparing the evening meal.

PRESENTS FOR LISA

The winter of 1862–1863 presented the Wheeler family with new challenges. With Pa away, they had far less money to live on, and they worried about where he was and when they would see him. The war made everyone anxious. When the Civil War began in April 1861, people said that it would be over in a few months. But the war had been raging for nearly two years now and there was no end in sight. And Tim was so tired from school, work, and helping out at home that he often fell asleep as soon as he had washed and dried the evening dishes.

In spite of the difficulties, everyone in the family was in good spirits. They were proud of Pa for joining the Union army, and they were proud of themselves for managing while he was away. By early December, Tim was busy making Christmas presents, especially for Lisa. Lisa liked games and Grandma Esther showed him how to make an African game called *mankala*. He also made a copy of a toy in Ma's store called the floating ball.

PROJECT THE FLOATING BALL

In the 1860s, toy companies began to make all sorts of simple, inexpensive toys, called "penny toys" because they cost a penny each. One of the most popular penny toys was the floating ball. While the original toy was made with a metal tube or a pipe, like the pipes used for blowing bubbles, you'll make yours out of a plastic drinking straw.

MATERIALS

1 flexible plastic drinking straw
scissors (manicure scissors or sewing scissors will work best)
ruler
1 pipe cleaner
transparent tape
2 or 3 dried peas or small piece of cork or Styrofoam (small cork balls are available in the toy or hobby section of many discount department stores)

1. Bend the short end of the plastic straw up so that it is at a right angle, as shown in the picture.

2. With the scissors, cut four small slits in the end of the straw closest to the bend. Each slit should be about ½ inch long.

3. The four slits make four flaps. Fold the flaps back, as shown, to form a nest or cradle for the ball.

4. With scissors, cut a pipe cleaner to a length of about 4½ inches. Bend one end of the pipe cleaner into a circle, as shown in the picture. Notice that you have to flatten this circle so that it will form a target above the straw. Make a small bend in the bottom of the pipe cleaner so it will fit around the bent flaps of the straw.

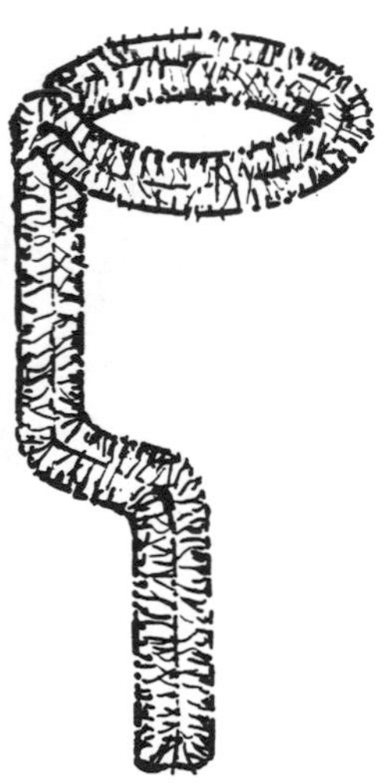

5. Attach the pipe cleaner to the straw by wrapping transparent tape around the straw and pipe cleaner, as shown.

6. If you can't find a small cork ball, use a dried pea (have two or three on hand, in case you lose one). You can also use the small scissors to cut a small ball out of a piece of cork or Styrofoam packaging material.

7. Place the pea or ball on the nest at the end of the straw. Blow gently and steadily into the straw and try to raise the ball up through the target circle and back down to the nest. After some practice, you'll be able to float the ball up and back on a cushion of air. The secret is to blow steadily and not too hard.

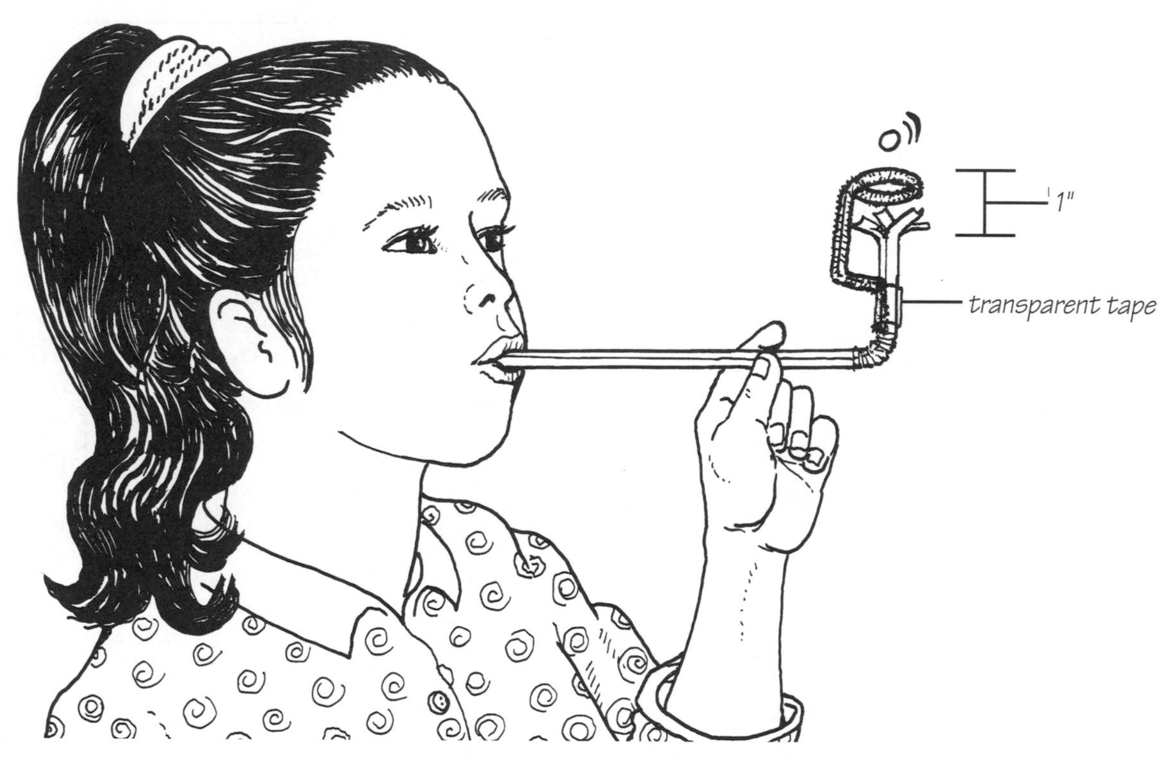

THE GAME OF *MANKALA*

Mankala is still played today in many parts of Africa, and there are at least a dozen different ways to play the game. In most versions, the players use polished stones as game pieces and play on a wooden board containing shallow grooves or cups. In this activity, you'll make your own mankala board out of an empty egg carton.

MATERIALS

1 empty cardboard or Styrofoam egg carton
scissors
transparent tape
48 small, clean pebbles or dried beans or seeds
2 players

1. Remove the lid from the egg carton. Cut off a piece about 3 inches long from each end of the lid. Use transparent tape to attach one lid piece to each end of the egg carton, as shown in the picture. These will be the home bins for the two players.

2. Place 4 pebbles, beans, or seeds in each of the 12 cups of the carton.

3. Players sit with the game board between them. Each player owns the six cups on her side of the board and home bin on her left.

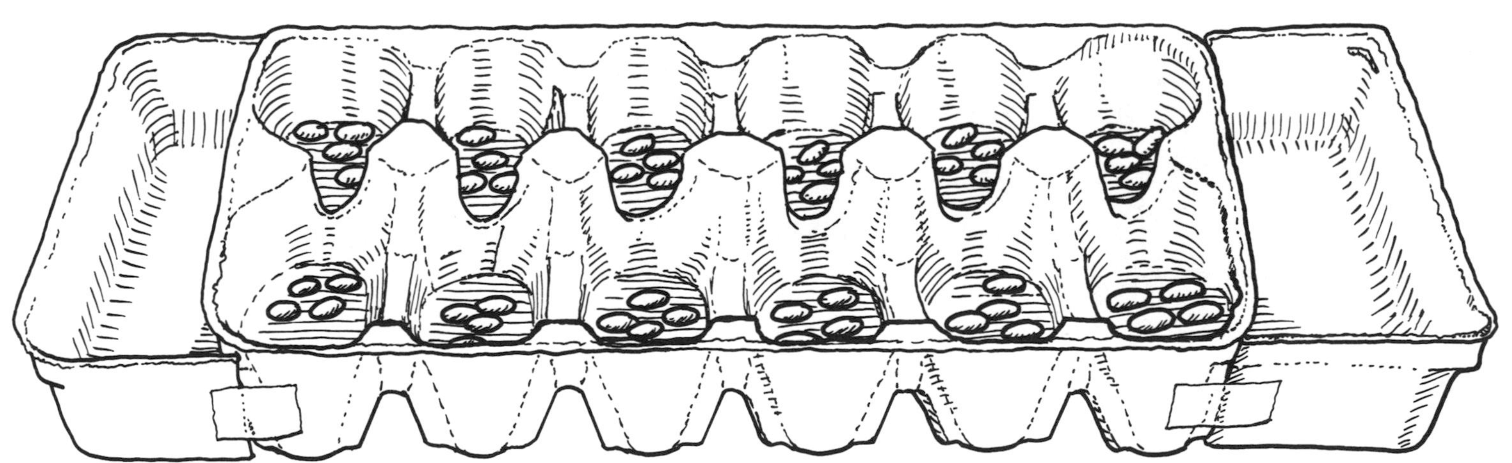

Toys: From Wood to Tin to Iron

Until about 1840, most children's toys were hand-carved of wood. Then new machines were invented for toy makers to manufacture toys out of thin pieces of tin. The tin toys were very popular during the 1850s and 1860s because the toy companies could add little windup springs that made the toys move. But the tin was so flimsy that the toys quickly fell apart or broke.

In the 1860s, something new emerged—toys made of iron. The iron toys were heavy and solid, but had no windup mechanism. Instead, they were built with wheels and children pulled them. From the 1860s through the early 1900s, iron toys were made by the millions. Children especially liked the iron transportation toys, such as circus wagons, fire engines, and railroad steam engines.

4. Use any method you wish to see who goes first. Player 1 removes all the pebbles from any one of her cups. She moves counterclockwise, dropping one pebble in each of the next four cups, including her own home bin, but not Player 2's home bin.

5. Any time Player 1's last pebble lands in an empty cup on her own side, she captures all of the pebbles in the cup directly across from the empty one, and places them in her home bin.

6. If Player 1's last dropped pebble lands in her home bin, she earns a free turn. (Of course, she'll have to have a lot of pebbles in a cup to move all the way around Player 2's cups to her home bin. But the number of pebbles in the cups can change several times during the game.)

7. The players continue to take turns, each taking all the pebbles from any cup on her side and dropping them one at time in the next 4 cups. As the game continues, the number of pebbles in every cup will change again and again.

Note: Players are not allowed to touch the pebbles in any cups in order to count them. The only time a player touches the pebbles is to play them.

8. The game ends when all six cups on one side are empty. The player with the most pebbles in her home bin is the winner.

A SPECIAL CHRISTMAS SEASON

The Christmas season of 1862 was an exciting one for the Wheeler family. They received a letter from Pa saying that he would be home soon after Christmas. The family also looked forward to New Year's Day, the day President Lincoln's Emancipation Proclamation would become official, declaring freedom for all slaves in the states still fighting for the Confederacy.

The whole family worked together to decorate the apartment for the holidays. The owner of Ma's store gave them a Christmas tree and lots of extra branches to use for decorations. Tim, Rachel, and Lisa made ornaments out of paper. They stamped some of the ornaments with a printed design, using stamps they carved from potatoes. Then everyone helped Grandma Esther turn some of the pine boughs into a big evergreen wreath to hang on the wall.

PROJECT EVERGREEN WREATH

The idea of decorating homes for the Christmas season developed slowly during the early 1800s. By the 1860s these decorations had become very popular, and magazines and newspapers offered ideas for decorating the tree, making special table settings, and using evergreen boughs to make wreaths. You can buy an inexpensive wire frame for your evergreen wreath at most discount department stores or at a florist's shop. (A wire frame is easier to work with than one made of Styrofoam or straw.) As a substitute for buying a frame, ask an adult to bend a wire coat hanger into a circle.

MATERIALS

about 2 dozen evergreen branches
pail
tap water
several sheets of newspaper
wire wreath frame
paper towels
scissors
thin, flexible wire, such as florist's wire (available in most hardware departments)
12 to 15 small pine cones
sprigs of red berries, such as holly berries, barberries, or cranberries (optional)
1 yard of red or plaid ribbon

1. Whether you buy evergreen boughs or cut your own (with permission, of course), it's a good idea to place them in a pail of water for a day or two before you begin. This will help keep the branches soft and easy to work with.

2. Spread several sheets of newspaper on your work surface and place the wreath frame on top.

3. Remove the evergreen branches from the water and dry the wood ends with paper towels.

4. With scissors, cut 2 or 3 small sprigs from one of the branches and cut a short piece of the flexible wire (about 6 inches). Wind the wire around the sprigs 2 or 3 times, then around the wire frame, as shown in the picture.

5. Repeat step 4 to add sprigs all the way around the frame. Turn the wreath over and add some sprigs to the back. This will fill out the wreath and cover any bare spots.

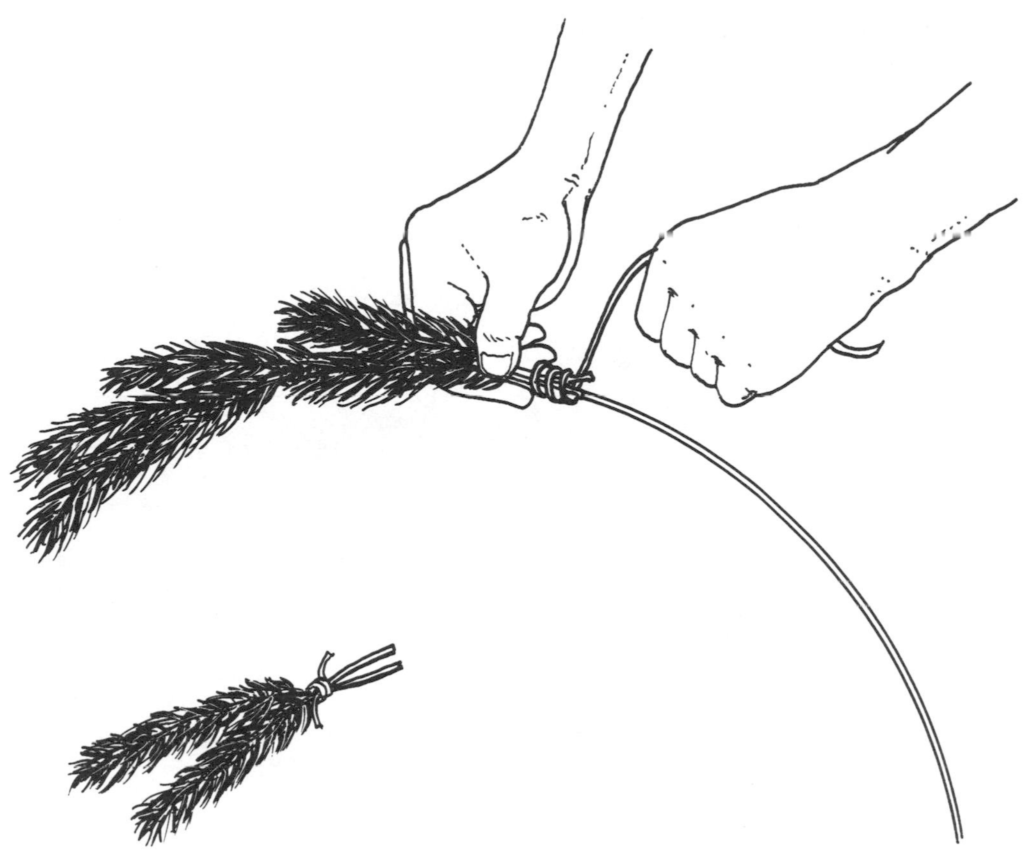

6. Sprinkle the pine cones with water. This will close up the petals and make the cones easier to work with.

7. Use short pieces of wire to tie the pine cones to the evergreen sprigs or to the wire frame. Space the cones evenly around the wreath.

8. For extra color, you can add some sprigs of red berries, tying them on with short pieces of wire.

From Saint Nicholas to Santa Claus

The original Santa Claus, called Saint Nicholas, came from the part of Europe that is now Germany. Saint Nicholas was a stern figure who would punish naughty children, but might give a piece of fruit to children who were good.

In the Netherlands, where he was known by his Dutch name, *Sinter Claes,* he was a much more kindly figure. Dutch colonists brought their Sinter Claes custom with them, and Americans translated his name as Santa Claus. In 1863, Thomas Nast, a well-known American artist and cartoonist, drew a picture of Santa Claus. Almost immediately, Nast's picture was accepted as showing what Santa must really look like.

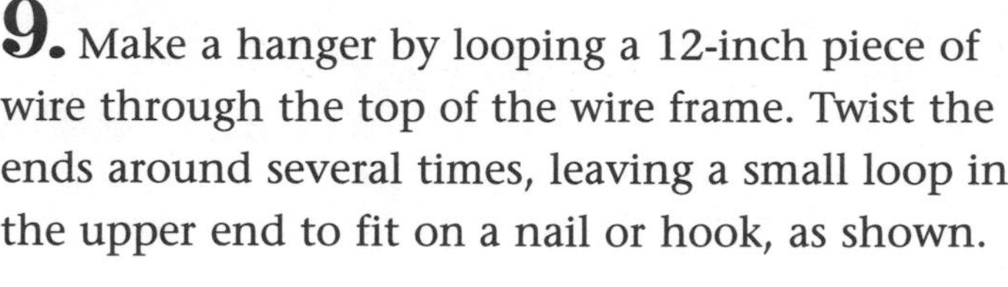
9. Make a hanger by looping a 12-inch piece of wire through the top of the wire frame. Twist the ends around several times, leaving a small loop in the upper end to fit on a nail or hook, as shown.

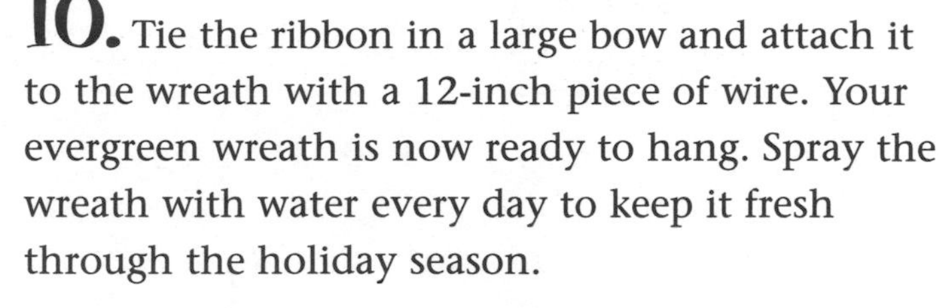
10. Tie the ribbon in a large bow and attach it to the wreath with a 12-inch piece of wire. Your evergreen wreath is now ready to hang. Spray the wreath with water every day to keep it fresh through the holiday season.

PROJECT POTATO-PRINT WRAPPING PAPER

With a printing stamp carved from a potato, you can decorate note cards, napkins, paper bags, or wrapping paper. Keep in mind that your potato printers will last for only a few days, so it's a good idea to plan all your printing for one or two days. If you need an extra day or two, wrap the potatoes in aluminum foil or plastic wrap and store them in the refrigerator.

MATERIALS

2 or 3 medium-size potatoes
paper towels
several sheets of newspaper
large, sharp knife, to be used by adult helper
black felt-tip pen with a fine point
paring knife or craft knife, to be used by adult helper
red, green, and yellow acrylic paints or poster paints
small paintbrush
scrap paper
white or brown wrapping paper
adult helper

1. Wash the potatoes and pat them dry with paper towels.

2. Spread several sheets of newspaper on your work surface and place the potatoes and other materials on top.

3. Ask your adult helper to cut the potatoes in half, making a straight cut so you'll have a perfectly flat surface. Two potatoes will make 4 stamps; cut a third potato only if you're sure you want 5 or 6 different stamps.

4. Blot the cut potato on paper towels to remove as much of the water as possible.

5. On the cut surface of one of the potato halves, draw the design for a stamp. Copy one of the designs shown, or create your own. If you make your own design, keep it very simple so that it can be carved easily.

6. The part of the potato that will print is the raised part, so have your adult helper use a paring knife or craft knife to carve away the part that won't print, as shown in the picture. The cut-away part should be ¼ to ½ inch deep.
Tip: The carving is easier if you cut away only a small section at a time. Blot the potato on a paper towel now and then to absorb the moisture.

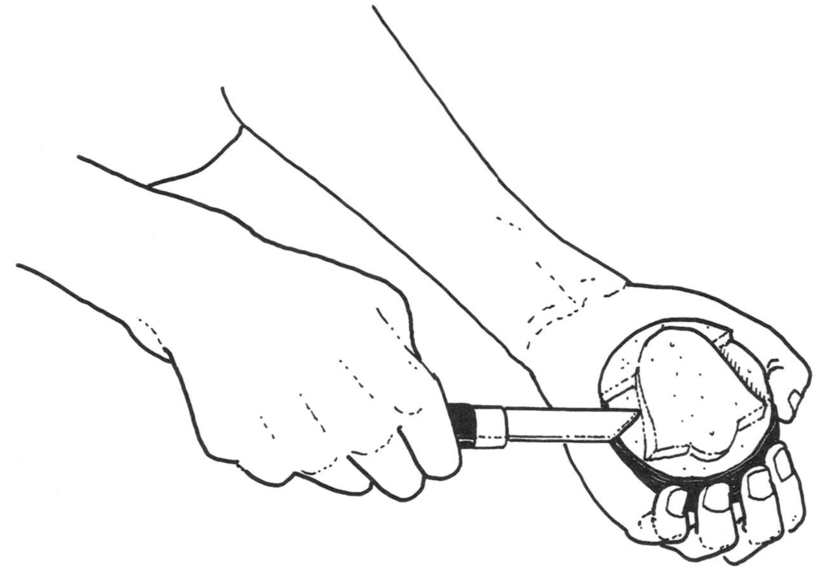

7. Blot the design part of your potato with a paper towel. With a small paintbrush, carefully apply a thin coat of paint to the raised portion of your design. Practice stamping the design a few times on a piece of scrap paper to get the feeling of how much paint to use and how much pressure to apply.

8. Repeat steps 5 through 7 for other designs you are going to use.

9. Place a sheet of wrapping paper on your work surface. Decide where you want to use each of your stamp designs. You can place them in rows, for example, or in circles, or in a random pattern. When you have in mind the arrangement you want, start printing. You can stamp all of one design first, then the others, or switch stamps after making two or three prints. Print as many sheets of wrapping paper as you need.

SERGEANT WHEELER

Solomon Wheeler arrived home two days after Christmas, proudly wearing the uniform of a sergeant in the 54th Massachusetts Regiment. The family was thrilled to see him, and so were all their friends and neighbors, who continually crowded into the tiny apartment to shake his hand. Pa told them all that the regiment would soon sail to an island off the coast of South Carolina to complete their training. The island was one of several captured by the Union army, who freed thousands of slaves living there. The North hoped to use the islands as a base for attacking Charleston, South Carolina.

The Wheelers and their friends held a joyous New Year's celebration. They attended a special church service, where the minister read President Lincoln's Emancipation Proclamation. He then led prayers for peace and for a final end to slavery in America.

Pa remained home through part of January 1863. He spent as much time as he could with Tim and Lisa. He helped Tim make a tumbling puppies toy for Lisa and a revolving serpent to hang above one of the kerosene lamps. And Tim showed off his cooking skills by making apple pandowdy, Pa's favorite dessert.

The Wheelers were both sad and proud when Pa left to join his regiment. Through the uncertain days ahead, they had the comfort of knowing that Sergeant Wheeler was helping to restore the nation and end slavery.

PROJECT APPLE PANDOWDY

Apple pandowdy was a favorite dessert in the 1800s, but no one knows how it got its name. The name may have come from the fact that breaking the crust makes the dish look a little messy, for the word *dowdy* means "messy" or "shabby." No matter where the name came from, apple pandowdy is easy to make and it's delicious served plain or topped with cream, whipped cream, or vanilla ice cream.

INGREDIENTS

ready-made pie dough for 9-inch pie (available in the refrigerated section of most supermarkets)
1 teaspoon cinnamon
¼ teaspoon grated nutmeg
⅛ teaspoon ground cloves
¼ teaspoon salt
8 large baking apples
4 tablespoons lemon juice
tap water
5 tablespoons butter
½ cup light molasses
cream, whipped cream, or vanilla ice cream (optional)

EQUIPMENT

large mixing bowl
mixing spoon
paring knife, to be used by adult helper
parer (optional)
small mixing bowl
wax paper or paper towel
pastry cloth or clean countertop
rolling pin
1½-quart casserole dish, or 13-by-9-by-2-inch baking dish
adult helper

MAKES

about 6 servings

1. Keep the pie dough in the refrigerator until you're ready to use it. Preheat the oven to 400 degrees F.

2. Measure the cinnamon, nutmeg, cloves, and salt into the large mixing bowl. Stir with a mixing spoon.

3. Have an adult help you peel and core the apples, and cut them into slices about ½ inch thick.

4. Pour about 1 cup of water into the small bowl and stir in the lemon juice. As soon as each apple is sliced, dip the slices in the lemon water. This will keep the apple slices from turning brown.

5. Place the apple slices in the large mixing bowl and stir well to coat all of the slices with some of the spice mixture.

6. Using a piece of wax paper or paper towel, spread about 3 tablespoons of the butter to coat the bottom and sides of the casserole or baking dish evenly.

7. Remove the pie dough from the refrigerator and roll it out on a pastry cloth or countertop with a rolling pin. Roll the dough into a shape and size that will fit the top of your casserole or baking dish.

8. Place the apple mixture in the casserole or baking dish, and pour the molasses over the top. Dot some of the apples with pieces of the leftover butter.

9. Lift the crust with your hands and place it on top of the apple mixture. Make sure the apple mixture is completely covered with the crust. If you have leftover dough, fit it around the sides of the casserole or baking dish.

10. Bake the apple pandowdy at 400 degrees F for 12 minutes, then reduce the heat to 325 degrees and bake for 30 to 40 minutes more. The pandowdy is done when the crust is lightly browned.

11. Ask your adult helper to remove the baking dish from the oven. Break into the crust with a mixing spoon, shoving some of the pieces down into the apple mixture.
CAUTION: The escaping steam is hot, so don't lean over the dish when you break into the crust.

12. Serve your apple pandowdy warm. You can serve it plain or with one of the toppings.

PROJECT REVOLVING SERPENT

In 1859, oil was discovered near Titusville, Pennsylvania. The oil provided Americans with a cheap fuel for lighting: kerosene. People quickly began using kerosene lamps instead of candles or whale oil lamps. Kerosene was not only inexpensive, it also gave a better light.

One small problem with the new lamps was that the rising smoke and fumes left a smudge on the ceiling. People solved the problem by using a simple toy that had been common for hundreds of years. Called a thermal toy, this was a simple metal or paper disk, divided into sections. When a thermal toy was placed above a lamp, the heat caused the disk to turn, or revolve. The revolving toy also collected the soot, and it was a lot easier to clean than a ceiling. The most popular thermal toy was in the shape of a snake.

MATERIALS

5-inch square of lightweight poster board or construction paper
pencil
scissors
crayons or colored pencils
white glue
pin or needle
about 24 inches of thread, white or black
transparent tape

1. Copy the design for the revolving serpent by drawing a series of spirals on the piece of poster board or construction paper. Notice that the tail is in the center and the head is on the outside spiral.

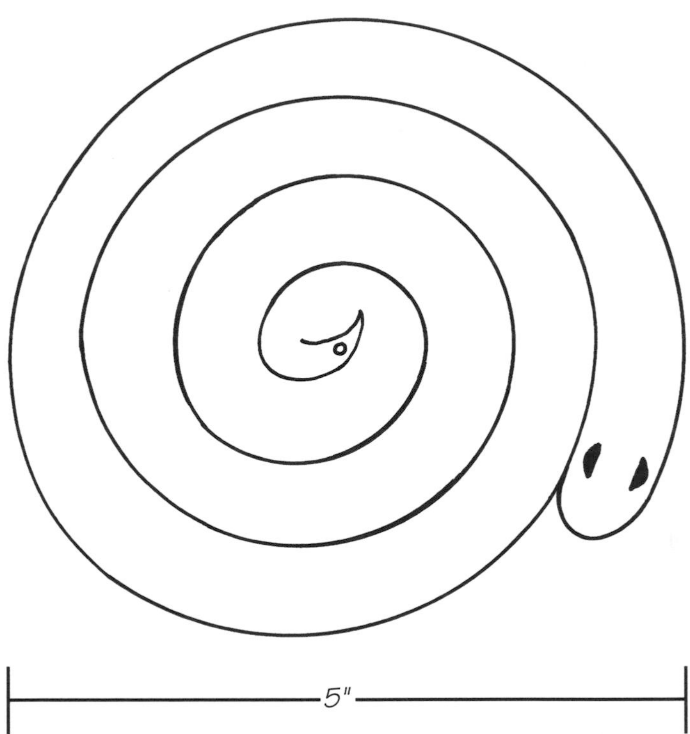

2. With scissors, cut out the serpent shape along the lines you drew.

3. Use crayons or colored pencils to decorate your serpent. Give it a pair of scary eyes and glue on a scrap of leftover paper to make a tongue. You can color the underside of the serpent too, if you wish.

4. Use a pin or needle to poke a hole through the tail. Push the piece of thread through the hole from the upper side of the snake. Tie the end of the thread in 2 or 3 knots so it won't slip out of the hole.

5. Hold the serpent by the thread a few inches above an electric light bulb. With the light turned on, the heat will rise and cause your serpent to revolve slowly. You can tie your revolving serpent above a lamp, or attach it with transparent tape.
CAUTION: Make sure that the serpent is at least 5 inches above the bulb to avoid any danger of fire.

New Year's Celebrations

When Dutch colonists settled in what is now New York State in the 1600s, New Year's Day was one of their most important holidays. The noisy Dutch celebrations included fireworks and the shooting of guns. Later colonists celebrated in quieter ways, some with parades, other with parties.

On New Year's Day 1790, the nation's first president, George Washington, and his wife Martha started a new tradition. They held an afternoon party, and instead of inviting only their friends, they welcomed everyone who wanted to come. This idea of a New Year's open house soon became very popular. Families placed announcements in newspapers, giving the hours of their open house. As guests arrived, they dropped a calling card in a silver tray. By 1860, some wealthy hostesses were competing with one another to see who could put on the most lavish party or collect the most famous calling cards. The party giving slowed down during the Civil War but revived rapidly after 1865.

PROJECT TUMBLING PUPPIES

Children in the 1800s were fond of toys that moved. One of the favorites was a simple tumbling toy that used weights to make an acrobat, a clown, or an animal tumble down an inclined board, very much like the tumbling puppies you'll make in this project.

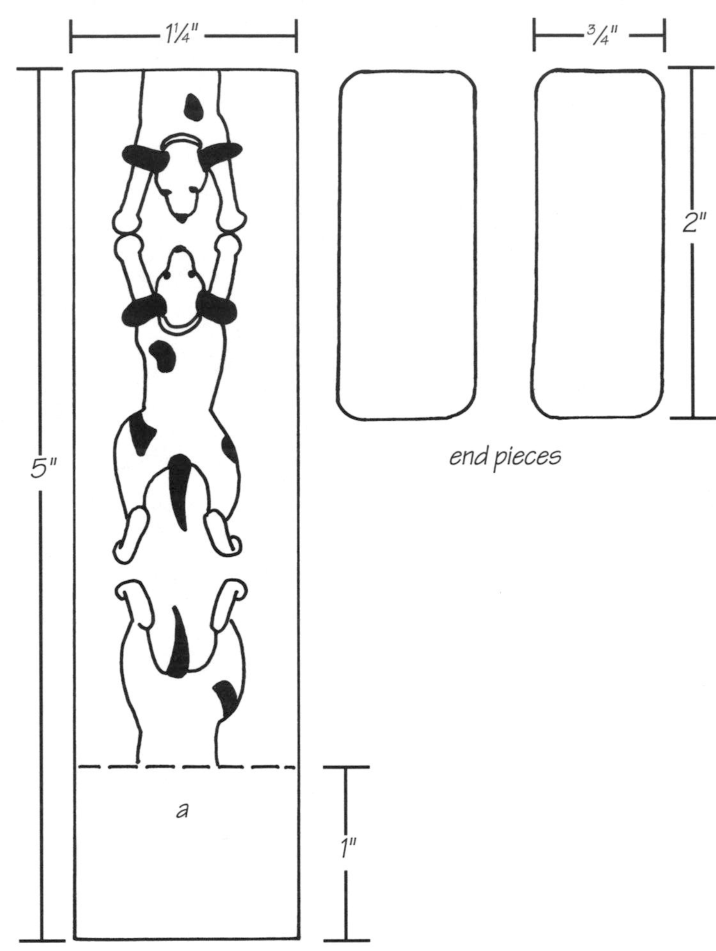

MATERIALS

poster board, about 4 by 6 inches
ruler
pencil
scissors
crayons, colored pencils, or felt-tip pens
transparent tape
2 marbles
board or stiff cardboard, 2 to 3 feet long and at least 4 inches wide
2 or 3 books

1. On a piece of poster board, use ruler and pencil to mark a strip 1¼ inches wide and 5 inches long. Cut out the strip with scissors.

2. Measure and cut out two smaller end pieces of poster board, ¾ inch wide and 2 inches long.

3. With ruler and pencil, mark an overlap line 1 inch in from the end of the 5-inch strip, as indicated by the dotted line *a* in the picture. On the rest of the strip, copy the puppies in pencil. Use crayons, colored pencils, or felt-tip pens to color the pictures in any colors you wish.

4. Bend the 5-inch strip back and forth several times to make it more flexible.

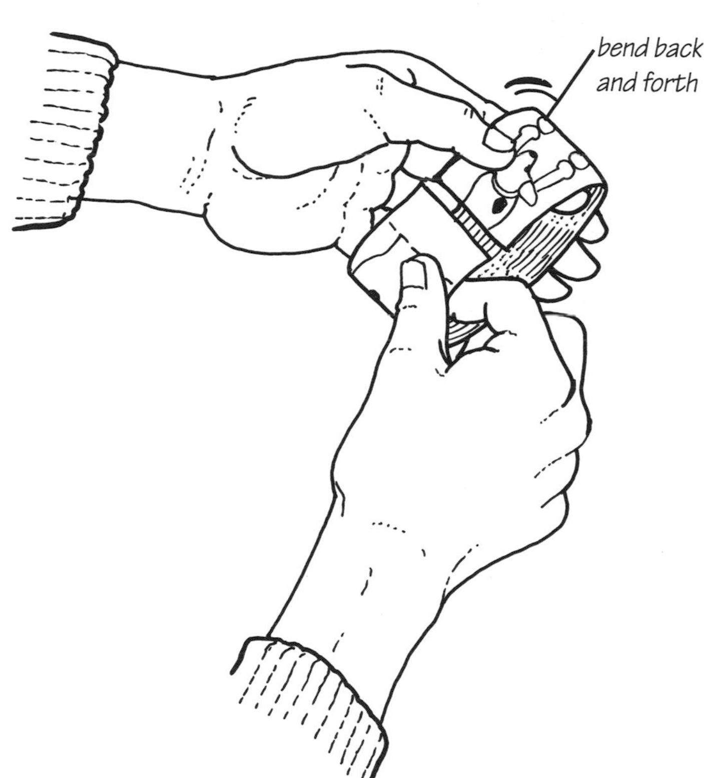

5. Fold the 5-inch strip over to make a loop, as shown in the picture. Overlap the ends and tape the two ends together.

6. Fit one of the end pieces to the looped strip and tape it to the strip, as shown.

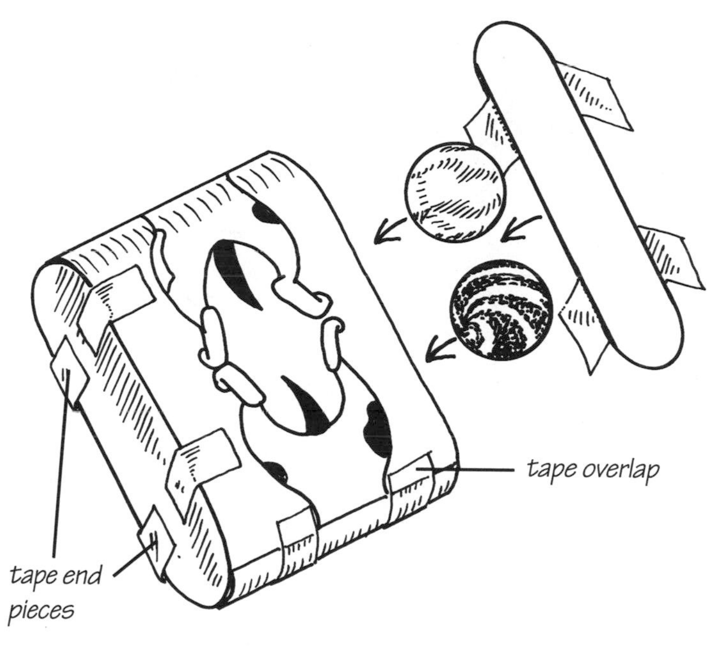

7. Place the two marbles inside and attach the other end piece with tape. Make sure all your seams are firmly taped so that the toy holds together and the marbles can't slip out.

8. Tip the board or cardboard at a gentle angle by placing 2 or 3 books under one end. Place your tumbling puppies toy near the top of the board, tip it forward, and watch it tumble down the board! (If the toy slides instead of tumbling end over end, the slope of the board is probably too steep. Adjust the board and try again.)

GLOSSARY

academy A private school, usually for girls and young women.

aeronauts Balloonists who soared in hot-air balloons over Confederate army positions to gain information for the North, forming the nation's first "air force."

***akwaba* doll** A small doll ornament or good-luck charm made in the kingdoms of western Africa.

Anansi The spider in western African myths who always outsmarted his bigger, stronger enemies.

Ashanti The peoples and cultures of several kingdoms in western Africa.

bandboxes Boxes made of thin wood or cardboard and decorated with wallpaper, used by travelers to carry personal items like gloves and hats.

cash crop A crop, like cotton, raised to be sold at market for a profit.

Civil War From 1861 to 1865, the war fought between eleven states of the South and the rest of the nation. The North's victory resulted in restoring the unity of all the states and ending slavery.

condensed milk Canned milk that has had much of the water removed by the process developed by Gail Borden.

Confederacy (or **Confederate States of America**) The name given to the new nation that eleven states of the South tried to form in 1861, leading to the Civil War.

Congressional Medal of Honor The nation's highest award for bravery in defending the country.

cotton gin A simple machine invented by Eli Whitney in 1793, which made the cleaning of cotton so much faster that cotton became a valuable cash crop.

Emancipation Proclamation The statement, or proclamation, issued by President Abraham Lincoln, declaring that all slaves in the states still fighting for the Confederacy would become officially free on January 1, 1863.

floating ball A popular toy of the 1800s, using a pipe or tube through which the player blows air to raise or lower a small ball.

forage To live off the land by finding food in one's surroundings.

Fort Sumter The U.S. fort in Charleston Harbor that was fired on by Confederate cannons in April 1861, marking the beginning of the Civil War.

gondola The basket underneath a hot-air balloon in which the balloonist rides.

Gospel music The songs developed by African slaves and free African Americans, presenting musical versions of Bible stories.

hardtack A hard, dry biscuit used by pioneers, sailors, and soldiers in the 1800s; also called sea biscuit, trail bread, and ship's biscuit.

hopscotch A game in which players hop on one foot through a pattern of numbered squares marked on the ground.

hot-air balloon A large balloon, filled with heated air, that could carry a balloonist hundreds of miles in humans' first success in flying.

immigrants People who move into a country from another part of the world.

jarabadash A popular African game, similar to tic-tac-toe, in which players try to make a row of three game pieces while also blocking the opponent from completing a row.

jazz A musical form developed by African American musicians in the early 1900s, incorporating traditional African rhythms and sounds.

kerosene A fuel developed from petroleum (oil) used for lighting, cooking, and heating.

King Cotton A term used to describe the importance of cotton in the economy of the South in the 1800s.

mankala An African game in which players move stones to different cups, each player trying to collect the most stones.

marzipan A very sweet substance, made with almond paste, used as pastry filling or to create miniature shapes for decorations.

Morse Code The dot-dash telegraph code developed by Samuel F. B. Morse and still used today.

mosaic A picture or design made by fitting small colored pieces together.

North The states that remained in the Union of States, or United States, during the Civil War.

pandowdy An apple-based dessert with a crust that is pushed down into the apple mixture after baking.

papier mâché A material made of paper strips or bits, mixed with paste, that can be formed into shapes that harden when dry.

Pennsylvania Dutch German settlers in Pennsylvania in the 1600s and 1700s, nicknamed from the German word for German—*Deutsch*.

penny toys Simple toys of the 1800s that sold for a penny each.

Pilgrims Early colonists from Europe who settled on the coast of present-day Massachusetts in 1620 and held the first Thanksgiving celebration in 1621.

plantations Large farms in the South that grew cash crops and used slaves as field workers and household servants.

Saint Nicholas The early name for the myth of Santa Claus, a stern figure but kind to children who were good, and perhaps named after a real Saint Nicholas who lived in the 400s.

scherenschnitte (sharon-SCHNIT-a) The German word for "scissor cutting," a technique for creating beautiful designs out of cut paper.

segregated Keeping one group separated from the majority group, as in the Civil War armies, in which men of African descent were separated from white soldiers.

shortbread A sweet, cookie-like cake.

short'nin' bread The name that developed for shortbread in many areas of the South, and still fairly common today.

Sinter Claes The name used by Dutch settlers for their Saint Nicholas and translated by other American colonists as Santa Claus.

South The name used to describe the eleven states of the Confederacy in the Civil War, and still used to describe the area south of Pennsylvania.

sutler A merchant who followed an army during the Civil War, selling food and other goods to the soldiers, from a Dutch word meaning "bad cook."

telegrapher A person who operates a telegraph by sending and receiving Morse Code messages.

thermal toy A toy that moves slowly when placed above a heat source like a lamp or stove.

Union The term used during the Civil War to describe the states of the North.

BIBLIOGRAPHY

The American Boy's Book of Sports and Games. New York: Dick & Fitzgerald, 1864.

Suzanne I. Barchers and Patricia C. Marden. *Cooking Up U.S. History: Recipes and Research to Share with Children*. Chicago: Teachers Ideas Press, 1991.

Josef and Dorothy Berger, eds. *Diary of America*. New York: Simon & Schuster, 1957.

Cobblestone, The History Magazine for Young People. 30 Grove Street, Peterborough, NH 03458.
Children's Toys, December 1986
America's Folk Art, August 1991

Marshall Davidson. *Life in America,* 2 vols. Boston: Houghton Mifflin, 1951.

Gwen Evrard. *Homespun Crafts from Scraps*. New York: New Century Publishers, 1982.

John Grafton. *New York in the Nineteenth Century*. New York: Dover Publications, 1980.

Alison Jenkins. *Creative Country Crafts*. Philadelphia: Running Press, 1994.

David C. King. *America's Story, Book 5: The Civil War Years,* 1850–1876. 2nd edition. Littleton, MA: Sundance, 1996.

John A. Kouwenhoven. *Adventures of America, 1857–1900. A Pictorial Record from* Harper's Weekly, New York: Harper & Brothers, 1938.

Nancy Lee and Linda Oldham. *Hands On Heritage*. Long Beach, CA: Hands On Publications, 1978.

Susan Milord. *Adventures in Art: Art and Craft Experiences for 7- to 14-Year-Olds*. Charlotte, VT: Williamson Publishing, 1990.

Eugene F. Provenzo, Jr. and Asterie Baker Provenzo. *Easy-to-Make Old-Fashioned Toys*. New York: Dover Publications, 1979.

Susan Purdy. *Festivals for You to Celebrate: Facts, Activities, and Crafts*. Philadelphia: J. B. Lippincott Company, 1969.

Reader's Digest. *Back to Basics: How to Learn and Enjoy Traditional American Skills*. Pleasantville, NY: Reader's Digest Association, 1981.

Carole Yeager. *Yankee Folk Crafts*. Dublin, NH: Yankee Publishing, 1988.

INDEX